The Politics of Management

Thinking Like a Manager

The Politics of Management

Thinking Like a Manager

COURSE GUIDE

Carleton University:
School of Public Policy and Administration

Masters in Public Policy and Administration

Richard Paton, M.A., M.P.A

Edited by Julia Paton, M.S., M.P.A

GSPH

GENERAL STORE PUBLISHING HOUSE INC.
499 O'Brien Road, Renfrew, Ontario, Canada K7V 3Z3
Telephone 1.613.599.2064 or 1.800.465.6072

http://www.gsph.com

ISBN 978-1-77123-051-3

Copyright © Richard Paton 2013

Cover art, design: Magdalene Carson

Printed by Image Digital Printing Ltd.
dba The IDP Group, Renfrew, Ontario
Printed and bound in Canada

Cataloguing data available at Library and Archives Canada

§

This book is dedicated to my late mother, Marie Paton, who inspired me to embrace learning and provided me with the capacity to embrace leadership roles. It is also dedicated to my dad, Martin Paton, who was my first example of a dedicated manager in his plant superintendent role at Ontario Hydro. Finally, it is dedicated to my wife, Julia, and our cherished children, Jasmine and Michael.

Contents

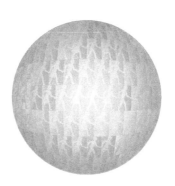

Preface

Origins and Purpose of the Politics of Management Course and Guidebook

This is a Guide and textbook for a course that the author has been teaching for the past twenty-five years: *"The Politics of Management: Thinking Like a Manager,"* Masters of Public Policy and Administration Program, Carleton University. It is a practical course, aimed at helping public administration students understand management on the ground. The course uses case studies and real-life experiences, applicable to both government and non-profit organizations.

Three major factors influenced the development of this course:

- First and most important, this course was specifically requested by students when the author was teaching an organizational behaviour course at Carleton University. Students wanted a "real" management course. I was requested to teach such a course and have been doing so for over twenty-five years.

- Second, the course represents thirty years of reflection over my career as a manager, starting as a policy director in the federal government and progressing to deputy secretary at Treasury Board and then to president of a business association, the Chemistry Industry Association of Canada.

- Finally, the overall approach to the course is inspired by my time at the Kennedy School of Government at

Harvard, which teaches executives how to deal with complex management situations through the case-study method.

Since my epiphany time at Harvard University, I have been continuously reading and learning about management and applying the best insights to my own management positions. To develop the course to its full potential, I have had to develop most of the cases, which are specifically designed to enable students to make management choices and utilize the concepts and framework of the course.

This is a guidebook. It is aimed to provide in one document the key concepts and framework and strategies for the *"Politics of Management: Thinking Like a Manager"* course, excluding the seven to nine cases that are part of the course discussion and related readings.

Right from its origins, this course was aimed at helping students in the first ten to fifteen years of their career how to assess management situations, work with managers, and manage in the complex reality of modern organizations.

After teaching nearly 750 graduate students over the years (mostly part-time and already working), it is very clear that young professionals in government—non-profit as well as private-sector organizations—face tremendous challenges learning how to work effectively in their organizational environment and developing their managerial identity. It is also evident from the student reviews of this course that a practical course like this is needed as part of a graduate program in public administration because (a) it helps students, in the initial part of their careers, understand the complex environments that managers face, and (b) it provides a path for students to learn how to become effective managers.

The aim of the course is to help students "think like managers" and to develop the basic diagnostic skills, as well as the potential to develop strategies and agendas to succeed in complex management situations. The course and this accompanying Guide focus on making decisions in a complex organizational environment faced with myriad relationships and issues.

The course is designed to complement other courses in MPA or MBA programs that tend to focus on functional areas of management such as financial management or human resources management; or policy courses focused on decision-making in public organizations. There are four major needs that I have identified over my many years of teaching:

- Understanding how organizations work and how they are managed

- Learning how to think like a manager: what the specific challenges are in a variety of organizations and the role of managers in meeting these challenges

- Developing the student's own managerial identity or approach to managing and leading groups or organizations

- Developing the capacity to devise agendas and strategies and implementing them in an effective manner

Organization of This Guidebook

This Guide is organized into five sections that follow the overall course outline. The first section focuses on the nature of management and key management challenges, especially for supervisors and middle managers. It also includes the key concepts and required insights into organizational dynamics. This covers the first four classes of the course and two cases that introduce students to the "thinking like a manager" approach.

In the second section, there is considerable focus on the organizational context and relationships that are important to developing effective management strategies, or networks. It outlines the "thinking like a manager" framework that is central to the course. The challenges of dealing with each of the major elements are described (i.e., manager; external environment; superiors; subordinates; clients; and other groups).

The third section focuses on the manager, which is at the centre of the "thinking like a manager" framework. This section outlines four critical choices that managers must make when developing their leadership style, including making decisions about agenda, teamwork, and their role and approach to organization and decision-making.

The fourth section draws together the overall lessons regarding the development of management strategies and outlines—what this author calls "death moves," or decisions, or strategies that make it almost impossible to manage an organization effectively. It includes some overall suggestions on how to develop oneself as a manager. It is most relevant to the final assignment, in which students must reflect on the overall concepts and assess what they have learned about management and about themselves as potential managers, or as individuals working with managers.

The fifth and final section includes some key attachments to the course, including the definition of key concepts; guidelines for doing case analyses; and, finally, guidelines for studying managers. These guidelines were developed several years ago for a research seminar taught by the author. The seminar involved the application of the concepts and the analytical framework of the Politics of Management course to study selected managers, who then would come to class to discuss their jobs. Through this course, about fifty papers have been completed on managers, and about twenty managers have come to class to share their experiences. This attachment is included because students may opt for this approach as a final project.

This guidebook does not use footnotes, and I have adopted the approach of referring to the author and publication in brackets throughout the text, as a more practical approach for this type of publication. More extensive and complete references are included in the attached bibliography.

Thank You!

In developing this Guide, I have had four major sources of support. First, thanks to my wife, Julia, the meticulous task of editing this book has been accomplished. Julia is also a Kennedy School graduate, and she has shared my enthusiasm for developing this course going back to the early 1980s. I have been fortunate to have her support all these years as I toiled away on this course.

Second, Charlaine Gendron has worked with me as my assistant as long as I have taught this course, over four different jobs—twenty-four years. Without her support, I do not know how I could have taught this course for so long. She also provided invaluable assistance in the final formatting of this Guide.

I also want to thank the hundreds of students who have taken my course and the feedback they provided. It is through the interaction of both teaching and managing organizations that I have been able to develop this course. By engaging students for so many years, I have been able to fine-tune the framework and concepts to maximize the effectiveness of this course.

Finally, I would like to thank the School of Public Policy and Administration at Carleton University, which has given me the unique opportunity to teach the same course as a sessional lecturer for over twenty-five years.

In particular, I would like to thank two directors of the School of Public Policy and Administration. It was Bruce Doern who originally agreed to my proposal to teach this course back in the mid-1980s. At that time, this course was only an idea. I continue to be grateful that Bruce endorsed this course experiment.

As director of the School of Public Policy and Administration over the past several years, Susan Phillips encouraged me, with a combination of charm and persistence, to return to teaching the course, after a brief absence. Susan has also encouraged me to develop this publication and to continue to develop this course as part of the public management stream of the MPPA program at Carleton University.

What Students Learned in the Politics of Management Course:

Quotes from Students

At the end of the course, students are asked to review it and reflect on what they have learned about management, their own career experiences, and their potential as managers. These are some of the quotes from previous students that provide insights into the value of this course. I have asked each of these students for permission to use these quotes. Other quotes are from the confidential course evaluations, and for that reason they are anonymous.

Students' comments

> I would like to conclude by saying that the Politics of Management course is a very practical and relevant course for policy students like me, as well as for anyone who is interested in learning more about managing modern organizations. I believe that the framework of analysis and the concepts learned throughout this course give me an advantage and offer me an opportunity to become an effective manager. While I believe that being a good manager is an art and not a science, I also know that it is an art a person can master by applying the lessons learned from the literature and case studies provided in this course. (Milana Simikian, 2012)

> Another interesting aspect of the course which I appreciated was the focus on the manager as a person, and how this impacts the roles, styles and choices which managers make in several key ways. . . . Cultivating an awareness

of your own preferences and tendencies as well as learning to identify (and even appreciate) different personality "types" and work styles in others is an essential component of learning to operate effectively in the "diverse and interdependent" environments that are typical of modern workplaces. (Morgan Goddard, 2012)

* * *

The fourth and final thing that I will take from the course, and arguably the most useful thing, is the models and approaches used to help organize chaotic situations into manageable ones. The first of these is the "Map of the Managerial Landscape" that we used to analyze the cases each week. This framework really helps to meaningfully organize information pertaining to the parties involved and their relationships to the manager, the nature of the environment in which decisions are being made and actions taken. (Morgan Goddard, 2012)

I have no doubt that this course and the concepts we learned and applied will influence my managerial style and inform my decisions as a future manager. (Kelly Cuan Edwards, 2012)

Even if I do not go into management, I think that the frameworks from this course are really applicable to life in general, as an employee, and outside my office. If one can understand the demands, constraints, and choices that they face in every situation, and determine what their greatest sources of power are to meet those demands, and nurture relationships and set goals, then decision making, and life, could run a lot smoother." (Stephanie Coady, 2012)

This course was extremely useful and relevant for my professional and personal aspirations. At its core, its value added is that it gives students tools, concepts and methodologies to approach the total environment of any given managerial situation. (Francis Nolan–Poupart, 2012)

The Politics of Management course taught me a great deal about the real-life situations and challenges faced by managers in the Canadian public sector. Although other program courses that have provided the theoretical and conceptual backgrounds on the government have been informative, I felt this course was particularly useful, especially as I saw opportunities to apply the course concepts in my professional life almost immediately. (Louise Grace, 2011)

The single biggest thing I think I will take from the Politics of Management course is the knowledge (even the reassurance?) that there is a structured approach to analyzing any new management challenge. The simple framework of evaluating manager/supervisors/subordinates/clients/others is a great improvement on my previous contemplations on management, which in retrospect have been something of a jumbled mess of questions. (Neil Misner, 2011)

* * *

This course taught me a lot about how to analyze a set of management relationships. It also gave me some tools for self-reflection and how this would shape my management style. (Neil Misner, 2011)

* * *

After a month into the course, I received a call from a manager at another department whose unit is similar to the one I work in. He was scouting a few leads for a replacement on behalf of his director. . . . Before taking this course I might not have thought to ask exactly the right questions and bundle them before going into the interview. I found this course helped my preparations a great deal. . . . And I was definitely better off for being aware of the nature of the challenge that making my first foray into management entailed. (Neil Misner, 2011)

"The Politics of Management: Thinking Like a Manager" course provided extremely useful concepts and case studies that were applicable to both professionals and those just beginning their career. The politics of organizational behaviour, learning to "manage up" and understanding the need to balance demands/constraints in your own position, as well as your larger network are definitely concepts I will take with me. I have recommended this course to everyone in MAPA . . . and several who aren't. (Lauren van den Berg, 2010)

Comments from course evaluations

If I knew two years ago what I have learned in this course about working with superiors and ensuring alignment of my agenda with others, I would still have my job at Immigration. (MBA student at Queen's executive MBA program).

I loved the practical nature of the course. The concepts are sure to be helpful for years to come.

This was the best course I have taken at Carleton. The concepts and framework for analysis were useful and practical. The Professor's experience and knowledge of course material was invaluable. I enjoyed the case study method and assignment format.

The approach to learning is very effective. There is a good mix of reading with case work. I agree that this is an excellent way to really learn to understand concepts and how to apply them.

These kinds of comments, which have been typical over the years, illustrate to me that the Politics of Management course is achieving its purpose of providing a practical management course that is relevant and useful to students of public administration and young professionals who are beginning their careers.

The feedback has encouraged me to invest in continuously improving the cases, readings, and class discussions. This Guide is one more step forward to improving the course by making the framework, concepts, and strategies outlined in the course even more accessible to students. This will enable students to focus on applying the lessons of the course to cases and examples of managers and managerial challenges.

SECTION I

Challenges for Managers and Key Concepts

1.0 Overview

How can managers manage in the context of increasingly complex organizations? How can they reconcile conflicting and diverse interests and get the job done? Are there ways that managers can increase their potential to develop and implement an agenda in an organization? How do they personally cope with demanding jobs and develop their managerial identity? These are some of the questions that face today's private and public sector managers. These challenges are even more extreme for first-time managers who are experiencing their first taste of supervising staff and working with superiors and others.

The title of this course, "The Politics of Management," stems from the essential challenge of management: to bring together conflicting interests in order to achieve the aims of the organization. The skills required to achieve this kind of organizational leadership are in most respects "small p" political skills of establishing a vision, mobilizing support, and building partnerships. The Guide places a particular emphasis on the challenges for first-time managers in developing their managerial identity.

The framework and concepts presented here are based on an extensive review of relevant management literature, several hundred studies of executives, my own research on the role of deputy ministers and chief executive officers (CEOs), my management experience of many years, and my time at the Harvard Kennedy School of Government. In addition, I have drawn on some important research by Linda Hill on the challenges of becoming a manager. This research is particularly relevant to the students of this course, most of whom are starting their careers and often working part-time in government or non-profit organizations.

This Guide helps students address some of these management and leadership challenges. It aims to provide a managerial perspective based on the realities of managing a modern organization and the challenges faced by managers in reconciling conflicting priorities and interests. Moreover, this Guide includes a practical management framework that will provide the focus for all readings, cases, research, and discussions in the course.

1.1   What Is Management?

Management involves getting the work of the organization done through other people.

The nature of management is closely linked to the nature of organizations. We define organizations, as Chester Barnard did in *The Functions of the Executive*, as

> ". . . a system of co-operative activities of two or more persons, something intangible and impersonal, largely a matter of relationships . . ." (p. 75)

According to Barnard, the distinguishing feature of organizations is that they are systems of activities composed of human beings who are co-operating. And to co-operate and work effectively, these people must develop certain structures, communications, and operations. It is the task of ensuring that the overall organization is working that Barnard calls executive functions, or the functions that are specifically "management" in nature.

In 1937, Barnard developed a definition of the executive functions that has stood the test of time and that is still relevant today. He wrote:

Executive work is not that of the organization, but the specialized work of maintaining the organization in operation. (*The Functions of the Executive*, pp. 215–17)

In other words, when a sales agent becomes a sales manager, his/her job is no longer selling cars or houses. The job is developing the organization, the incentives, and the framework to help sales agents sell cars or houses. Even though they may engage in some non-executive work, their primary job is to "maintain the organization," or to ensure that the system within which sales agents work helps to achieve the organization's objectives. This lesson, as Linda Hill has explained in *Becoming a Manager*, is the most difficult lesson for first-time managers to learn.

Barnard described three executive functions that are critical to any organization:

- Formulate and define purpose (this is essential for linking staff to the overall direction of the organization).

- Provide a system of communication (enabling staff to understand what is expected).

- Secure essential efforts (enabling staff to contribute to the organizations). Barnard's view was that employees had considerable power simply by not giving their best, or by not linking to the organization's objectives.

Barnard also indicated that the executive, as head of an organization, has an obligation to find the proper equilibrium or balance between the organization and the external environment.

Rather than engage in the fairly tiresome distinction between managers, executives, and leaders, I will simply use the term manager to mean those individuals at supervisory, middle, and senior levels who have a responsibility for mobilizing and guiding organizations and their staff. Also, I will use the term managers, leaders, and executives interchangeably throughout the Guide.

Henry Mintzberg, who is recognized as one of Canada's global gurus on the subject of management, has done an excellent job of pulling together the views of various authors on management in his recent book, *Managing*. Following are a few quotes from that book.

On the distinction between management and leadership

Frankly, I don't understand what this distinction means in the everyday life of organizations. Sure, we can separate leading and managing conceptually. But, can we separate them in practice? Or, more to the point, should we even try? (p. 8)

How would you like to be managed by someone who doesn't lead? That can be awfully dispiriting. Well, then, why would you want to be led by someone who doesn't manage. That can be terribly disengaging; how are such "leaders" to know what is going on? As Jim March put it: Leadership involves plumbing as well as poetry. (p. 8)

On the role of the manager

Managing takes place on three planes, from the conceptual to the concrete: with information through people and to action directly. (p. 49)

We might thus characterize the manager's position as the neck of an hourglass, sitting between a network of outside contacts and the internal unit being managed. (p. 30)

Managers frame their work by making particular decisions, focusing on particular issues developing particular strategies, and so forth, to establish the context for everyone else working in the unit. (p. 50)

Mary Parker Follet wrote in 1920 that "the test of a foreman is not how good he is at bossing, but how little bossing he has to do." (p. 215)

On the authority and style of managers

What you do as a manager is mostly determined by what you face as a manager. (p. 13)

While every manager has to make the job, he or she also has to do the job. That is why managerial style cannot be considered out of context, independent of where it is practiced . . ." (p. 13)

When a specialist becomes a manager, the biggest change often is (or should be) the shift from "I" to "we." Having become responsible for the performance of others, the first instinct, as Hill found out, is to think, "Good, now I can make the decisions and issue the orders." Soon, however, comes the realization that formal authority is a very limited resource of power and that to become a manager is to become more dependent on others to get things done. (p. 65)

Mintzberg in *Managing*, also quoting Hill in *Becoming a Manager*:

Management has just as much, if not more, to do with negotiating interdependence as it does with exercising formal authority . . . being a manager means not merely assuming a position of authority but also becoming more dependent on others. (p. 65)

Summary

Managers are responsible for the total organization and their job is to provide direction to that organization, create meaning for staff and stakeholders, help establish the fundamental purpose and agenda of the organization, and enable the people and groups in the organization to work effectively and efficiently to achieve the purpose of the organization.

The manager's role is, however, deeply situational. It depends on the challenges facing the organization. The role of the manager often can involve the full range from strategy and policy and external relations to operational details, if they are relevant to achieving a successful organization.

The major challenge that first-time managers face is defining their role and agenda in the context of the specific situation, and to develop a managerial identity and style that is both appropriate to their strengths and personality and that is required in a given managerial situation. This is the subject of the next section.

1.2 The Unique Challenges of Supervisors and Middle Managers

This section describes the unique challenges of supervisors and middle managers in a range of organizations. There are three examples provided: a policy director, a head of an enforcement unit, and a general manager of a golf course. These examples will be used throughout the Guide. In addition, this section describes the results of the general research on the challenges of transition to middle manager jobs.

Jacob Martin, director of policy: Aboriginal Affairs

Jacob Martin is a respected senior policy advisor who has developed some important policies and cabinet documents. He is the senior officer in a group of sixteen policy analysts and administrative staff. He has six years' experience in a government organization and a Masters in Public Administration with a focus on policy. When his director is promoted to director general, Jacob assumes that job.

Although Jacob has little management experience and is not too comfortable with the idea of being a manager, he wins the job due to his knowledge of the policy area and his capacity to develop briefings and presentations for senior management and stakeholders. He was also recognized for his capacity to work with teams of policy analysts and other groups. As a director with a staff of sixteen, Jacob begins to recognize that he has made a huge transition and that he needs to learn what it means to be a manager. Unfortunately, like most first-time managers, he is going to learn on the job, in the midst of significant challenges that involve new areas of expertise such as managing relations with superiors, developing a budget and allocating resources, and dealing with staff performance issues, etc.

Diane Lavoie: manager enforcement, Fisheries

Diane is a senior fisheries officer in the Maritime region who has demonstrated superb skills at working with fishers and negotiating with clients and other groups. After five years in this position, she is promoted to be chief of fisheries enforcement, reporting to a director general who has overall responsibility for regulatory affairs and intergovernmental co-operation.

In moving from this role as a fisheries officer and working with teams on specific projects, she is now responsible for a group of twelve enforcement officers, many of whom have twenty years or more experience than her, and some who are close friends. What kinds of challenges is she going to face moving into this position? How can she best establish her role while maintaining a strong and effective group? How will she wrestle with the personal challenges of balancing her work and family life and coping with the deficiencies she will inevitably face in doing this job?

Ronald Storie: general manager, Heritage Golf Course

Ronald is a golf professional with a degree in business and golf management. He has been a successful golf professional at the Heritage Golf course, responsible for managing a golf shop with four staff. When the general manager is fired because of poor organizational skills and poor member relations, the club decides to appoint Ron to the job. Ron is keenly aware of the fact that over ten years there have been six general managers, only two of whom were considered competent and successful. One moved to another club, and one left due to illness. The others were "let go" at the end of the golf season.

What kinds of challenges is Ron going to face in making this transition? He will now be responsible for the overall physical management of the course, the clubhouse, and the food and beverage facility, as well as golf operations. Instead of just four golf professional staff, he will now have all of these groups reporting to him and he will report directly to a board of directors and the president of the board.

These kinds of transitions are not easy and can be treacherous to those who are not able to adapt and learn the new requirements of the job.

The challenges facing these three managers are very typical in government organizations and, on a smaller scale, in non-profit organizations. According to Linda Hill, this is the most difficult transition that managers face because it requires them to move from the role of an individual contributor to that of managing an organization. Unfortunately, there is not an easy bridge to these new roles as managers, and many people find they are facing a very different set of challenges and skills than on their previous jobs.

Generally, new managers form a managerial identity in their first couple of jobs, and their approach does not change substantially over their careers. Judging from the experiences of many of the students in the Politics of Management course and discussions with a range of executive coaches, many managers in government and non-profit organizations are facing huge difficulties dealing with their jobs, and many arrive at a managerial position long before they are ready to take on that challenge.

Managers who cannot adjust to these new roles face severe personal challenges. Their inability to manage their jobs also results in a range of counterproductive tendencies such as: micro-managing to the extreme; lack of team building; poor relations with superiors; inability to develop agendas; and difficulty managing relations with other groups. This results in the creation of dysfunctional organizations, which creates conflict and stress for staff and a lack of innovation and productivity.

Employees who have worked in a hostile, conflict-ridden, stagnant organization with a terrorizing boss know the toll that it can take on staff. Those who have experienced a superb and caring working environment with strong leadership and excellent morale, teamwork, and performance will remember those organizations for years as the best places they ever worked.

Unfortunately, there are far too many organizations where managers cannot cope with their jobs and end up creating a negative environment, eroding potential performance, undermining the development of staff, and jeopardizing the success of the organization.

Since many of the students who take my course at Carleton University recognize that at some point in their careers they could be in supervisory or middle-management positions, or at least work with such managers, it is important to explore why this transition is so difficult and what it means to the forging of a managerial identity.

There is little research on the challenges faced by middle managers in public organizations, but fortunately, there has been some excellent work on private sector organizations that is relevant to both non-profit and government organizations. Linda Hill has written two significant books on this subject and has developed many cases. The first book is *Becoming a Manager: How New Managers Master the Challenges of Leadership*; it is a study of first-time managers and the challenges they face in the first two years on the job.

Hill's work is extremely relevant to the needs of students taking the Politics of Management course. Most of the research was focused on private-sector executives who made the transition from individual contributors (e.g., car salesman to sales manager). As the three examples above illustrate, managers in government and in non-profit organizations face the same types of challenges.

Five key challenges for supervisors and middle managers

Based on the experience of the writer and the above research, there are six major challenges faced by supervisors and middle managers. These challenges are all outlined in the superb *Becoming a Manager* book by Hill. This Guidebook highlights five of the challenges that Hill mentions.

(i) Recognizing the complexity, uncertainty, and demands of the job

As the head of a unit, a manager comes face to face very quickly with the fact that he is the pivot point between his group and his superiors and other groups; and he must deal with the overall environment facing the organization, which is usually complex with many issues. His job is to manage up and out and at the same time manage the overall work of his group. Hill explained this with these words:

> Managers have to juggle diverse, often ambiguous, responsibilities and are enmeshed in a web of relationships with people who often make conflicting demands: subordinates, bosses, and others inside and outside the organization. As a result, the daily routine in management is often pressured, hectic and fragmented. (pp. 13–14)

(ii) Defining one's as a manager

The hardest part of the transition from individual contributor as a program officer, salesman, or policy analyst to supervisor or manager is to define one's role and where one can add value to the organization. This is where the quote by Chester Barnard really becomes useful. Managers need to define their role in terms of maintaining the organization, not doing the work of the organization. They need to define their role in terms of how they balance the external environment and expectations of superiors with the need to secure and engage their staff in achieving the purpose of the organization. Linda Hill found this to be the case in her research.

> The new managers generally defined their new positions by their responsibilities, not their relationships. Starting out as new managers they did not appreciate the distinction between being primarily responsible for people rather than the task. . . . All new managers were uneasy about managing relationships with superiors and peers. (p. 21)

(iii) Understanding the limitations of authority and how to lead organizations

One of the surprises that first-time managers and supervisors find is that once they get to be the boss, the authority of the position does not equate to significant power and influence. As a result, they have to find other ways to lead their groups and achieve the results required.

As John Kotter has illustrated in his book *Power and Influence*, the complexity, diversity, and interdependence of organizations often means that the key groups that are required to achieve an agenda are outside the authority of a manager. Managers have to find ways to mobilize their organization to achieve results. Linda Hill, in her research on first-time managers in their first year on the job, described the challenges these managers faced in her book *Becoming a Manager*.

> The managers did not realize that they were confronting a basic reality of managerial work: that management is as much a position of dependence as a position of authority. They had to learn to lead by persuasion and not by directive. (p. 100)

> During their first year the managers became aware of some of the major principles in exercising authority: establishing credibility, building subordinates' commitment, and leading the group. . . . They still had much to learn about how to exercise power and influence; now that they understood some of the principles, they had to implement them. Exercising power and influence, especially without relying heavily on formal authority, is a challenge for even the most seasoned managers. (pp. 111–12)

(iv) Managing themselves: dealing with the stress of learning a new function and the inherent conflicts in the job

Linda Hill has also found that most first-time managers go through a very difficult period developing their managerial identity, which involves a lot of soul-searching about their capabilities, difficulties in terms of time management, and challenges in dealing with conflicts or expectations of staff. For many of these managers, it took at least a year to become comfortable in the role and to know how to carry out the job.

Through their experience, they had to learn to reframe their understanding of what it meant to be a manager and feel competent in their new role.

> The managers not only struggled with anxiety about their performance, but they also grappled with what it felt like to be undergoing a change of identity. They reported feelings of marginality, of being betwixt and between. They found "changing from" as traumatic as "changing to." . . . the promotion to manager was a mixed blessing because it forced the managers out of the specialty with which they identified. They lost their sense of mastery and of who they were. (pp. 177–78)

(v) Developing the required understanding of the political or relationship-building requirements of the job and capacity to manage

One of the major challenges faced by supervisors and middle managers is recognizing that there are "political" aspects to their jobs that involve networking and relationship building.

Hill summed it up this way:

> To succeed, most of the new managers acquiesced to their "political" responsibilities. They acknowledged that they should devote time and energy to developing relationships with those outside their unit. (p. 83)

> As they became aware of and accepted both their agenda-setting and network-building responsibilities, they began to recognize just how right they had been during their first days on the job. Time management, ability to set priorities, and decisiveness were critical managerial skills. Now . . . the challenge they faced was more complex. First, they

had to be able to set the agenda for their unit, to ensure that they were focusing on the things that were the most important . . . Second, they had to manage the tradeoffs, a very delicate balancing act among their responsibilities. (pp. 79–80)

Hill researched the prime qualities that are required to make the transition from policy or program officer to supervisor or manager:

From interviews I was able to identify the prime qualities the managers saw as part of managerial character: self-confidence, willingness to accept responsibility, patience, empathy and ability to live with imperfect solutions. Most said such factors of temperament were critical in making the transition successfully. (p. 167)

In addition, Hill notes that the development of this capacity occurs mainly through the experience of doing the job. In essence, they became managers through the experience of managing.

There is some preparation that can be done to ease this transition from individual contributor to manager. However, it is likely, based on Hill's research, that managers have actually to go through this experience completely to understand and be comfortable in a managerial role. This transition—as we will see below with Diane Lavoie, Jacob Martin, and Ron Storie—is not just cognitive learning. It involves carrying out new roles and developing the emotional strengths required to manage an organization.

One of the great contributions of Hill's book is that it helps managers going through this transition understand that they are in good company, and that they can make this transition smoother by learning from the experience of other first-time managers.

Middle managers in the public sector

One of the observations by the author in his article on middle managers, "Middle Managers: Upscale Supervisors or Emerging Executives," in the Canadian federal government was that they had to recognize that in making the transition to managers, they were no longer expected to be technical experts.

They were required to understand the environment they worked in, the realities facing superiors. Moreover, they had a responsibility to develop an agenda and direction for their group that was realistic and achievable within the context of their organization. In other words, they had to recognize that there is a "small 'p' political" side to their job involving building relationships and developing support for an agenda or direction.

The Paton research on middle managers shows that public sector managers face many of the same challenges as first-time managers in the private sector. Public sector managers face the challenge of managing interdependence within and without their organizations, perhaps in an extreme form.

Public sector managers had to recognize that they had to manage their relationships with superiors in a way that helped their boss to achieve their objectives and, at the same time, enable their own organization to meet their objectives.

Prior studies have addressed the complex accountability affecting Canadian deputy ministers in relation to, for example, the prime minister, the ministers, central agencies, etc. This is illustrated vividly in Osbaldeston, *Keeping Deputy Ministers Accountable.* Junior managers face similar complexity and uncertainty in their working environments, as they depend on many different groups. However, their authority is often very limited.

Like senior executives, junior managers need to follow the advice that Kotter has outlined in *Power and Influence,* of developing an agenda, building a network of support, and implementing that agenda through the network. As the author explained in his article on middle managers, junior managers, too, need to think like executives and manage their environment in order to achieve their agenda.

As an absolute minimum, managers at the chief and director level need to understand the environment that top executives face and endeavour to build relationships in order to achieve their superiors' and their own agenda.

The Paton article also illustrates that the political environment of government, the pressures of dealing with the public and the press, and other considerable constraints are not limited to senior executives such as deputy ministers. A program manager, or a regional director general in, for example, Aboriginal Affairs and Northern Development, or Fisheries and Oceans, also requires a lot of managerial, leadership, and networking skills to manage their environment and achieve their objectives.

> Middle managers will continue to have to learn how to manage in an uncertain and complex environment. . . . The more senior executives focus on working with ministers, parliamentarians, and external groups, the more important middle managers will become to carry out program and departmental management functions in the context of the overall policy directions and agenda of the minister. . . . To manage in this environment, middle managers will be required to develop the strategic perspective, environmental sensitivity, and broad understanding of departments and government that is usually associated with senior executives. (Paton, *Middle Managers*, p. 259)

Summary

Managers and supervisors can be successful in meeting the challenges of their new positions if they understand and accept the inherent complexity and difficulty of the job; define their role as manager as distinct from a program officer or policy advisor; understand the power relationships and decision-making in their organization; forge a managerial identity; and develop the capabilities and emotional intelligence required to lead their group.

Jacob Martin, as a recently appointed policy director; Diane Lavoie, as a new manager of enforcement; and Ronald Storie, as a general manager of a golf course, will all likely face the challenges that Linda Hill and Paton identified.

Before becoming general manager of the Heritage Golf Club, Ronald Storie has only managed a pro shop with some staff; now he is responsible for managing all aspects of a golf course, including areas where he has little experience or credibility. He also is taking on a job where the failure rate is astounding. He will need to quickly develop his managerial identity and define his role. Unfortunately, as Hill has described, he will be doing it while on the job with the board of directors and members, as well as staff, looking over his shoulder.

Given the lack of serious management training in most public organizations, and the lack of support or advice for managers who struggle with their roles, there are far too many instances where managers face serious difficulties doing their jobs and are never successful in a managerial role.

A manager who is struggling with his or her job is not pretty. This can result in serious problems for organizations and particularly for the staff. It also can create havoc in the lives of these new managers who are just not comfortable in their jobs and never quite feel that they have a "handle" on how to carry out their role successfully.

The Politics of Management course is designed to improve the capacity of students to:

- Understand what management involves

- Analyze the organizational environment and power relationships

- Think like a manager and develop a managerial identity

- Determine the best way to develop an agenda or strategy for carrying out particular management jobs—especially in their first supervisory or management job

1.3 How Do Organizations Work? A Managerial Perspective

To be effective as a manager, one has to understand how organizations work. Because management takes place within a specific and changing context, it is very difficult to rely on general theories to guide managerial behaviour. The history, culture, structure, environment, decision-making process, and players in each organization are different. In fact, the same organization might operate quite differently over a period of a few months.

A manager needs to know the factors, or influences, that can shape a particular organization and its decision-making processes and recognize certain trends or patterns. The executive has to, in effect, put together his/her own analysis of the organization, based on the factors at play, and has to understand how he/she interacts with the organization. The organization may be analyzed from three different perspectives:

- The overall dynamics of the organization as a whole, its environment, and its systems

- The key relationships among the groups and players within the organization

- The major issues, events, or decisions the organization faces, often within a relatively short time period

This Guide will briefly describe these three levels of analysis and their significance for managers and executives. In addition, readings in other areas of organizational behaviour, human resources, and organizational change may also be relevant. This course, however, will be focused on what these concepts mean in practical terms to the executives who have to lead and direct such organizations.

Overall dynamics of the organization and its systems

To best understand the overall dynamics of an organization, students should refer to John Kotter's *Organizational Dynamics*, which explains the six key elements required for analysis. The chart in that book is an excellent reference for understanding these factors. This chart will be included in the readings for the course.

- Environment (external and task)

- Dominant coalition

- Employees and other tangible assets

- Formal organizational arrangements

- Social systems

- Technology

(i) Environment

Kotter describes the environment as including two aspects:

    a.   The external environment
    b.   The task environment

The external environment is the broader context within which the manager and the organization must operate. It could include the economy, the political environment, societal values, relationships with other governments, etc. The task environment refers to the key suppliers of resources (Kotter, *Organizational Dynamics*, p.12). This would include funding organizations, those that are integral to delivery, and those in a relationship of direct interdependency such as in, for example, immigration and the RCMP, which must co-operate in the delivery of border services.

There is a wealth of research (Lawrence and Lorsch, *Organization and Environment*, p. 209) that illustrates the need for organizations to interact with their external and task environments, and organizations have to be designed to respond to these requirements. As Barnard noted many years ago, the role of the manager is often to determine how best to balance external requirements with the goals of the organization for which they are responsible.

(ii) Employees and other tangible assets

This dimension includes factors such as the size of the workforce and the nature of the assets of the organization—land, infrastructure, tools, and money (Kotter, *Organizational Dynamics*, p.14).

The range can vary widely among organizations. For example, a department of national defence can have tens of thousands of employees, dozens of locations in the country and overseas, and literally billions of dollars in equipment, some deployed abroad. Compare this to a central agency that has a few hundred staff, is located in one building, and has as its major material assets computers and computer systems. Likewise, their dynamics and their challenges will vary widely.

(iii) Organizational structure

This element refers to the formal organizational arrangements and systems that shape the operations of the organization. This includes the division of labour, hierarchy, and operational systems (Kotter, *Organizational Dynamics*, p.15). Kotter argues that organizational structures and systems can have a major impact on organizational dynamics. This is why it is so critical for managers to understand the structure and systems of their organization, and their likely impacts on the available options. One part of understanding the organization is the degree of differentiation and integration as defined by Jay Galbraith in *Designing Organizations* (Appendix A).

(iv) Social systems

The social system, according to Kotter, is the culture and social structure of an organization (Kotter, *Organizational Dynamics*, p.18). Organizations develop cultures and values that lead to the establishment of social systems, where groups sharing a common perspective work together more easily than groups that have a different background and organizational culture.

(v) Technology

Kotter defines technology as the techniques, or approaches, that the organization uses to achieve its objectives. He does not define technology as machines or equipment, but more in terms of processes. For example, the technology for a central budget agency may include: the review of submissions, the development of policy, the establishment of budgets, and controls for departments. This is very different from a fisheries department that allocates quotas for fishing and enforces regulations in the field; or a revenue department that processes millions of tax filings and interprets the application of the tax code.

(vi) Dominant coalition

This element is extremely useful and important for managers to understand. Kotter defined it basically as the: "minimum group of co-operating employees who oversee the organization as a whole and control its basic policy making." (Kotter, *Organizational Dynamics*, p.20)

To identify the dominant coalition, one needs to look at the major decisions made by the company, department, or association and ask who had to be involved and provide support.

Most of the time, the dominant coalition includes the senior people in the hierarchy, but not always. For example, sometimes the minister and chief of political staff take on the major policy role and allocate implementation to the deputy minister. In this case, even the deputy minister might not be critical to the dominant coalition for overall policy decisions. In other situations, it might be the deputy who is the real power broker, and the minister is content to focus on a few areas of interest and focus on his constituency.

In non-profit organizations, the key members of a dominant coalition are usually on the executive committee, or are prominent board members who represent key organizations. In some cases, however, a person will be part of the dominant coalition because they are able to articulate approaches to policy and gain support for their position.

In governments, managers are continuously assessing power relationships to understand who is shaping the decisions and how the various players interact. This is essential to determine if a cabinet document will "fly" or not.

The organizational dynamics components developed by Kotter are not new. What is really useful is how he puts them together into a framework that helps managers understand how organizations work.

The idea that these elements, in the medium term, will need to be in alignment, or achieve some sort of equilibrium, is a very significant insight. Managers can use this understanding to determine how to respond to issues when becoming aware of a major non-alignment.

If an organization faces a major change in its external environment there will be a non-alignment with the organizational structure, social systems, or other elements. This will require, through a chain reaction, that some adjustments be made to maintain alignment.

Take, for example, Research in Motion (RIM). It faced a major market shock in 2012, as Samsung and Apple developed their hand-held phones with many more applications. This eventually put a strain on the unique co-management regime of the company, required a change of the dominant coalition to a new leader, and brought about serious changes to the organizational processes involved in product development and the product itself. By 2013, they had made a lot of adjustments and launched new products to try to re-establish alignment with the market. By 2013, the stock price had somewhat recovered. At least, the company did what it had to do to realign with the market environment. Time will tell whether they were successful or were too late.

Another example might be a government organization that has a very strong culture and social system linked to established professions and universities. Or one that is wedded to a particular approach to implementing environmental or health policies and is based on strong government intervention, complex federal regulations, and lengthy processes. This culture may have little sensitivity to economic realities, economic development, and job creation.

With new governments and changes in political direction, senior management reporting to ministers may face significant challenges balancing the culture, expertise, and advice offered by incumbent officials. The government may want a more streamlined approach to regulation, more provincial versus federal leadership, and higher priority for economic and resource development. This could create a major non-alignment with the leading officials and social system in a department. Unless the department adapts quickly, the minister will either have to appoint new senior managers, or drastically change the traditional practices and policies of the organization.

So, the reason that Kotter's framework is so useful to the Politics of Management course is that it provides a way of understanding the dynamics of organizations, and it can be easily used by managers to assess their management challenges and the areas they will need to focus on to be effective.

This Guide is designed to provide only the bare essentials that students require to analyze organizations and understand how to manage better within an organizational environment. This brief introduction is aimed to help students assess the context of the major cases in the course; it is within this organizational context that managers must develop and implement their chosen strategies.

To oversimplify this fascinating area, there are seven factors that must be continuously taken into account in analyzing an organization and developing various strategies for management.

All of these aspects of organizational behaviour must be understood within the context of the specific organization and its relationship to a particular unit or group.

- Assessing the External and Task Environment

- Determining the Power Structure and Decision-making processes.

- Identifying the Key Dependency Relationships

- Understanding the History and Culture of an Organization

- Knowing the Incentives that Drive Behaviour

- Analyzing the Forces for and Against Change and Leverage Points

- Understanding the key decisions, and the dynamics surrounding those decisions. These decisions can enhance or undermine the agenda of a manager.

Summary

There is a wealth of literature on all of these aspects of organizational behaviour, including excellent books on organizational culture, decision-making, dependency relationships, etc. It is not the purpose of this Guidebook, however, to provide a course on organizational behaviour. The key elements provided by Kotter in his *Organizational Dynamics* book will provide a sufficient foundation for the assessment of management challenges and the development of strategies to meet those challenges.

The three managers we described earlier—Jacob Martin, policy director, Diane Lavoie, fisheries manager, and Ronald Storie, golf club manager—will all find that, in their jobs, they must understand their organization and its relationships with key stakeholders and the environment.

If, for example, Diane is facing very hostile fishing groups, due to dwindling stocks and prices, the enforcement challenge is going to be very different than if all these groups are happy with their business and the department. She may require more support from superiors than normal, and the skills and capacities of the team might be quite different than if relationships with fishing groups were healthy and stable.

To succeed in his job as a manager, Ronald Storie will have to really understand the dynamics of the Heritage Golf Club and the key factors that lead to the persistent firing of previous general managers. He has to find a way to perform and meet the expectations of the board.

For Jacob Martin, a policy group usually is linked to the overall agenda of the department as derived from the minister, the deputy minister, and the overall government agenda. To do his job well, Jacob will have to understand the overall dynamics of the department and interface with the Aboriginal groups. It might be sufficient for a cabinet document to get the support of the minister, but if the government and the prime minister have a clear preference, it will be critical further to understand the dominant coalition with respect to that issue.

All three of these first-time managers will enhance their capacity to be successful if they can understand their role and the dynamics of the organizations. This is why understanding organizations and how they work is so essential to effective management.

Power mapping for managers

In addition to the broad systems that shape the organization, a manager must take into account its structure and division of labour and its authority and power structure and identify the key players or dominant coalition.

As various authors have pointed out (Richard Cyert and James March, *A Behavioral Theory of the Firm*, p. 27), organizations are usually made up of coalitions of interests and can often be best understood by analyzing which coalition has the dominant influence at any given time or on a particular issue.

Thus, from a manager's viewpoint, it is very important to analyze how the structure, as well as the key players and groups, can shape an organization. If, for example, an executive committee is dominated by a deputy minister and assistant deputy ministers who more or less share a common philosophy and approach, then it is likely that they will make most of the decisions. However, political leaders, especially after an election, might have a very clear agenda as well. In this case, the main drivers of change will be these elected leaders, and the role of the public service would be to implement their proposed changes.

In a private sector firm, for instance, there might be tremendous differences among the executives on strategy, policy, or operations. If these strong sources of power counterbalance each other, the company will inevitably face a crisis of decision-making, including erratic decisions that are incompatible with a consistent approach.

The Politics of Management course aims to develop skills to analyze power relationships in an organization, understand the major dependency relationships, and identify the levers that a manager can press. This type of analysis, or "power mapping," is the focus of one of the first two cases of the course.

To establish and implement an agenda and get the job done, the executive must understand the organization and its players and be able to assess with some degree of accuracy the probability of support for a given course of action. An executive who constantly pursues an agenda, only to be thwarted by other players or by circumstances that he has failed to take into account, will soon lose credibility, as well as the ability to influence superiors, colleagues, and subordinates.

At this point three concepts must be discussed: authority, influence, and power.

Authority

Authority is the right to make decisions, or take action, as the person responsible for an organization or group. It is usually conferred to a position and can involve a variety of activities, such as establishing a budget, hiring staff, reviewing performance, signing off on contracts, or correspondence, etc.

Authors such as Kotter argue that the authority of most positions in complex organizations is not sufficient to achieve a management agenda. Managers and organizations are usually dependent on many other groups and individuals over whom they have no authority. He also argues that managers are dependent on staff for their commitment, expertise, etc. and that authority is not sufficient to elicit the required commitment to achieve an agenda.

Influence

Influence can be loosely defined as the capacity to have an impact on the actions or behaviour of others. In his book *Power and Influence*, Kotter illustrates the myriad ways managers employ to influence others: personality, credibility, expertise, vision, appeal to self-interest, and even humour (pp. 78–92).

Kotter also argues that since most positions do not, and cannot, have sufficient authority, there will be enormous power gaps in any job involving a complex organization; that is, the gap between the required power to establish and implement an agenda and the power that the manager actually has.

For this reason, managers must develop exceptional abilities to exert influence in order to overcome their dependency on superiors, colleagues, other organizations, and even on staff. As a result, Kotter also argues, in both *Power and Influence* and *The General Managers*, it is in the area of influence where most of the focus should be for executive development. This will be further explored in the last section of this Guidebook.

Power

Power is often defined as the ability of Person A to get person B to do something that person A wants done, or, among organizations, the equivalent. Power can combine both authority and influence and possibly other factors. The successful exercise of power can be observed and measured by determining whether person A was able to get person B to take a particular action, even if person B did not agree or was not interested. If Person B was not subject to the authority of Person A, this would be a clear illustration that this was the exercise of power and not authority.

J. Pfeffer (*Power In Organizations*, pp. 97–135) illustrates many of the sources of power in an organization, which may include control of scarce resources, management of uncertainty, provision of expertise, and control over defining alternatives. One of the first cases in the course focuses on power mapping for a regional director.

Power can often be seen as a negative concept, as in the brutal regime of Stalin or Hitler, or the abuse of power by governments or individuals. In organizations, there are certainly managers who through manipulation, loyalty, fear, divide-and-conquer techniques, and even sabotage can wield power for their own self-interest or aggrandizement. In these cases, having sufficient power does not contribute to a healthy or innovative organization.

In this course, power is a neutral concept related to the capacity of a manager to develop and implement an agenda in complex organizations. The exercise of power in the Politics of Management course is aimed at achieving the attributes of effective organizations, as described in section 1.4, above.

Summary

Developing the power to define and implement an agenda is essential to management in complex organizations with high dependency relationships, and the inherent conflict that occurs in diverse organizations.

Jacob Martin, as a new policy director, will need to quickly understand where the power lies in the department, and what the major priorities are. Is it the minister who is driving the agenda? Is it the Aboriginal groups? What roles is the deputy minister carrying out—trusted policy advisor to the minister, or policy-taker from either the minister or the prime minister? Is this issue part of the overall government agenda and that of the prime minister? Is there a consensus on the problem and a clear path forward, or are there major differences of views among the key players?

As a policy director, especially a newly appointed one, Jacob has to do his own power mapping and be ready to determine his agenda and approach in relation to these factors.

A couple of examples illustrate how important it is for managers to understand the power relationships in an organization. In one federal department, a DG of Communications was known as a "yeller." She constantly berated staff with a loud and aggressive voice and created a hostile and fearful organizational environment. At one point, thirty staff signed a petition asking for her to be replaced and sent it to the deputy minister. The deputy minister did nothing. Apparently, he had concluded that she was doing a good job; and was not inclined to make hard personnel decisions anyway. Clearly, the staff overestimated their power and did not appreciate how the deputy minister would respond.

A similar situation occurred when the senior management of the RCMP petitioned the prime minister concerning the management style of the commissioner. All of the senior staff eventually lost their positions before the commissioner changed. The commissioner outlasted all of them because, clearly, the government was not yet ready to make the change and had their own reasons for keeping him.

These two examples show how easily it is for managers to misunderstand the power relationships in an organization. The focus of the discussion of power in this course is to learn to offset the inherent power gaps present in most modern complex organizations, and enable good managers to get the job done.

Managers and the decision-making process

One of the key ways in which managers can shape organizations is by developing a clear agenda supported by the key players, understanding the decision-making process, and using all their influence to ensure that decisions enhance the achievement of their agenda.

One useful reference that helps explain how organizations make decisions is *Agendas, Alternatives and Public Policies* by John W. Kingdon. His analysis is consistent with other authors who found that some organizations tend not to be goal- or objective-oriented. In some cases, many other forces, other than the pursuit of specific objectives, have an impact on the work (e.g., history; professional orientation; avoidance of uncertainty; desire to maintain autonomy; etc.). Hence, it is important for executives to understand what tends to drive the organization in order to manage it.

Kingdon also argued that to understand decision-making, four relatively separate streams must be taken into account: problems, solutions, participants, and opportunities. Sometimes, the relationship between these factors is not clear. As Kingdon states:

> Some participants will actually fix on a course of action and cast about for a problem to which it is a solution, discarding problems that do not seem to fit. (p. 91)

In his case studies, Kingdon also noted that the four major streams often flowed separately, and that movement of the agenda often occurred when these streams came together either by chance, or by design.

> Once we understand these streams taken separately, the key to understanding agenda and policy change is their coupling. The separate streams come together at critical times. A problem is recognized, a solution is available,

> the political climate makes the time right for a change, and the constraints do not prohibit action. (p. 93)

When problems, solutions, policies, and politics come together, there is what Kingdon calls a policy window, of which policy entrepreneurs can take advantage—just like a space window (Kingdon, p. 204).

From a managers' point of view, Kingdon's analysis describes a real and immediate aspect of management. It is clear that to achieve their agenda, executives must be on top of highly current information, know the views of the various players, and understand the coupling of key streams of activity.

The organizational entrepreneur is able to take advantage of events to promote an agenda. The executive who is constantly missing the signals and who has timing problems in presenting his/her proposals will have limited success. One of the qualities of very successful deputy ministers is this ability to influence the decision-making process in government in the midst of complex political and bureaucratic dynamics and complicated processes involving cabinet and ministerial decision-making.

The same is true of managers in non-profits or the private sector. Those who can assess the total environment and trends and bring together pertinent key decisions, at exactly the right time, can develop power and influence. This is how reputations are built and careers made.

One of the most useful and unknown books on public sector management is by Gordon Chase, *How to Manage in the Public Sector*. This book was developed by a fellow student in the Kennedy School of Government in 1981. After the untimely death of Chase in a car accident, Elizabeth Reveal developed this book based on lecture notes. Chase, who was an accomplished manager in Washington and New York City, taught management from the point of view of a manager leading an organization having to deal with politicians or mayors, central agencies, the media, and other organizations.

The work of Kotter and Reveal/Chase bring an incredibly realistic assessment of management with a rare ability to articulate the craft of management and provide real insights into what it takes to be successful.

These two quotes illustrate the insight that Chase brings to the subject:

> Managers operate in a highly political and complex environment. Managers who produce are managers who have learned to turn internal and external relationships to their advantage: who know how to anticipate conflict, promote their agenda, and earn the professional respect of varied and diverse associates. Failure comes often to managers who have not mastered this environment, or taken its pitfalls and perils seriously. To understand this environment requires an appreciation of who the players are and why they are important. (p. 16)

> Other players can affect the manager in a number of welcome and not so welcome ways. They can provide or withhold necessary clearances, authorizations, and approvals on budget, personnel, procurement, or regulation—that determine whether programs will flourish or wither. They can provide political support, or they can turn political power against a manager's agency and program. And they can co-operate actively and participate in a program's management and operation—through volunteer services, donation of time and skills, or organize grass roots opposition to a manager's goals and strategies. Determining who is likely to do what, to whom, and when, is a skill as well as a talent. (p. 17)

Successful executives try to manage the process of decision-making to bring together key forces in an organization (e.g., problem; choices; opportunities; participants) and promote a given agenda. They will work to define or frame a problem in a certain way to assist the agenda. They will ensure certain players are involved to support a certain direction. They may limit various choices or shape alternatives to help their own cause. In government, if they are able to develop a strong synergy with their minister and chief political advisor in a department, their chance of success is greatly enhanced.

Osbaldeston (*Keeping Deputy Ministers Accountable*, p.85) has a chart that illustrates the complex nature of decision-making in government through a diagram that puts the minister and deputy minister at the neck of an hourglass, managing an agenda up to the prime minister and cabinet, out to various key groups, and down to the organization and department for which they are responsible. This chart will be included in the readings for the course.

Osbaldeston also argued that when ministers have a common agenda with senior management and the political staff, their chances of success are significantly enhanced. This is also a good example of the development of power in complex and uncertain situations. By aligning agendas with key department leaders and the overall agenda of the government, the ability to achieve that agenda will be considerably improved and the power gap will be dramatically reduced.

It is important that middle managers, or first-time supervisors in public organizations, understand the agendas of the key leaders of the organization and how they are working together or not co-operating in achieving this agenda.

Based on research with ministers and deputy ministers, Osbaldeston (*Keeping Deputy Ministers Accountable*, p. 90) notes that a major source of difficulty for ministers is their inability to develop a strong, coherent agenda aligned with the key players.

The very same kind of assessment could be done in terms of the relationship between a particular proposal in a private company and the overall direction of the top executives, or strategy of the corporation. A proposal that moves the corporation strategy forward and is aligned with the CEO's mandate will have a much better chance of success than one that is seen to be associated with aspects of the business that the company wishes to sideline or eliminate.

Case example: Jacob Martin

As a new policy director, if Jacob Martin is able to understand how streams of decision-making come together, determine how a particular policy proposal fits with the agenda of the government, minister, and deputy minister, and then identify the opportunities to move forward a policy agenda, he will increase his chances of success.

In an environment with many different coalitions of interests, whether it be government, corporations, or associations, an executive has to work hard at understanding key events and issues and determining how to take advantage of the convergence of issues and opportunities to promote his/her agenda.

1.4 Creating Productive, High-Performance Organizations

The business and management literature is full of studies that outline the requirements for effective organizations. As new managers take on their roles, it is very important that they have a good idea of the key elements that make organizations successful.

There is no doubt that the realities of working in government and non-profit organizations are very different from those in the private sector. An effective manager must completely understand the nature of the organization where he/she is working, and the specific requirements of managing in that environment.

The knowledge of the organization and its systems and the informal relationships one develops over the years can be a huge advantage in developing and implementing an agenda. For that reason, knowledge of the business is a very important factor. But the core challenges are very similar in public, private, and not-for-profit organizations.

There are as many differences within each of these three sectors as there are among them. Running a small, high-tech software company frequently developing new products is totally different than running an established railway or a shipping company. In government, managing the Department of Defence is surely very different than Aboriginal Affairs or the Health department. Finally, even within the non-profit sector, there are huge differences among these organizations in terms of size, membership, policy direction, etc. that definitely affect the management approach.

To manage in a given situation is necessary to understand the unique nature of that situation and organization, reviewing how it meets the key criteria for effectiveness; then, determining the best management strategy given the realities of that situation.

Regardless of whether one is managing in government, in a private company, or in a not-for-profit association, the key elements of the job are the challenges of:

- Providing direction for an organization

- Developing the required support and commitment to achieve the objectives of that organization

This Guide is focused on the essential challenges and choices that managers must make to ensure that the organization is productive and effective. The perspective of this course is that every organization has its own history, culture, and dynamics, and a good manager has to figure that out and then develop a management approach so that he or she can create the most effective organization possible.

Successful organizations have certain characteristics that managers will need to strive to achieve if they want to accomplish its mission and build a good team.

The article "No-Name Management for the '90s" by this author and Agnes Jelking outlines seven requirements for successful organizations in the public and private sectors (*Optimum*, Summer 1994, pp. 35– 41). These attributes were derived from an analysis of public and private sector literature on management, leadership, and organizations. These features are still valid today.

There is general agreement on the key attributes of the well-performing organizations. Thus, rather than creating still one more management panacea or buzzword, the authors presented these as elements of a "no-name management" approach, and argued that we should focus on the consistent application of these basic principles, as opposed to the continuous reinvention of approaches to performance assessment.

Thus, good organizations, according to the no-name management approach, must have:

1. *Clear mission, vision, and strategy.* The literature on companies illustrates that companies that have a clear view of their role and, particularly, their strategy in a highly competitive market, are the most successful.

   Jim Collins has written a fantastic book titled *Good to Great*. He shows that those companies with a relentless focus on establishing the right mission or strategy and achieving that mission succeed while others can disappear very easily. The challenge of having a clear mission, vision, or strategy is difficult in the private sector due to changing markets and technology and the capacity of leadership to make adjustments when strategies are not successful. In government, there are even more challenges in creating a consistent direction. The changes in government, ministers, and senior personnel can result in constant adjustments to the directions of departments that make it very difficult to provide a coherent focus and direction.

   Notwithstanding these challenges, managers of organizations have to determine the core purpose and direction for an organization and then ensure that the organization works to achieve that direction.

2. *Strong and effective leadership.* Organizations are usually more effective when the leader is able to provide the direction and achieve results. This does not mean that the leader has to be an egocentric "heroic" manager, but there are certain basic requirements of leadership that make organizations successful. Jim Collins's book also notes that the most successful leaders he has observed are amazingly humble and also believe strongly in a top-notch team approach to decision-making.

Providing direction and a sense of purpose, and building the required team required for the organization to be successful is the essence of leadership and management. Managers must be able to provide this kind of leadership but also to be able to assess themselves and their capacities and make the adjustments necessary to their strategy and their own style, depending on the requirements of the organization and its situation.

3. *Efficient structures and networks.* Most modern organizations recognize the importance of a strong financial management function, or information technology, and recognize the need to adjust organizational structures to meet changing needs. To address their challenges, companies have created single IT, human resources, and financial platforms for operations around the world. So, it is naïve to think that there is huge flexibility in large, global companies. Achieving this kind of uniformity is a major challenge for managers in global corporations.

   Like large corporations, governments are complex and require some uniformity and consistency, sometimes to the point of being counterproductive. Generally, governments do create constraints, rules, and procedures that are incredibly difficult to deal with, such as staffing, purchasing, contracting, reporting to Parliament, etc. A lot of these rules and processes are driven by the public nature of government and the requirements for accountability. One of the major challenges for public sector managers is to deal with these constraints but get the job done. This sometimes involves some creativity and the ability to challenge the purpose and approach to rules and practices. It definitely requires a good understanding of these requirements and the people responsible for administering them.

   Thus, whatever the organization or sector, managers have to learn to work with the organizational structure, systems, and networks that exist and shape them, where required, to achieve their agendas.

4. *Commitment and involvement of employees to perform their functions productively.* In private corporations that are successful, employees are committed to the company, and the leaders of the organization know how to build and strengthen that commitment. As far as the author has been able to determine, all surveys addressing workplace morale in government departments indicate major challenges.

    The nature of government with continuous change, political dynamics, serious constraints, and constant turnover of managers can easily undermine commitment of staff to the public service. When private companies begin to fail financially, the morale issues that emerge are serious. Keeping a strong committed and focused staff in these circumstances is very challenging.

    Regardless of the sector, managers have to figure out how to build a quality team and maintain the focus and commitment of staff to the organization.

5. *Clear client focus and efficient quality services and products.* In the private sector, if you do not serve clients with either products or services, you basically disappear as a company. The history books are littered with examples of companies that have missed the boat with clients or customers, while others have thrived. Jim Collins in his book *Good to Great* provides examples of these. Providing services in government is also challenging—whether it be getting a passport, an old age pension, or a driver's licence, or working with regulators on product approvals.

    Managers must be able to assess the quality of the service their organizations provide and their distinctive value and to understand how their organization contributes to the quality of services and products. Then, they must be able to lead the organization into making the required improvements.

6. *State-of-the-art management support systems to ensure their continued performance.* The importance of the

administrative and management systems needed to support effective organizations is often underestimated. Unfortunately, these systems are often described as overhead, as opposed to essential functions to achieve the organization's mandate.

The great companies that Jim Collins describes develop superb human resource development policies to ensure that their companies excel. Companies like Fed Express or Wal-Mart have developed IT systems for inventory, shipping, and logistics that are very important to their competitiveness. In government, the financial, personnel, IT, and other systems are also essential for high performance.

Unfortunately, in large public sector organizations, there are so many factors shaping these support systems that they often end up being overly centralized and process-oriented and lose sight of their essential purpose. For example, government contracts as low as $25,000 require time-consuming open bidding for transparency, and the staffing process gets mired in so many factors that getting the right person for the job becomes almost a subordinate priority.

It is essential for managers to understand these support systems and how they can help to achieve organizational objectives. It is also essential to manage their intrinsic constraints and work effectively with staff in these support functions, if one wants to be effective as a manager.

7. *Capacity for continuous learning and innovation.* This last attribute is discussed in the literature on learning organizations. Given the rapidly changing environment that most organizations face today, it is necessary to have the capacity to learn and innovate on a continuing basis. Again, Jim Collins found in his book *How the Mighty Fall and Why Some Companies Never Give In* (pp. 21–22) that organizations that fail typically ignore the signs of problems and just do not respond and learn.

Managers of organizations must be ready to learn continuously about what makes their organization tick, what makes their team effective, and how to generate innovation and success. This also requires them to be able to reflect and learn about the effectiveness of their management approach and what adjustments might be required in various situations.

Case examples

To effectively lead a high-performance organization today, managers must learn how to develop these attributes in government, non-profit, or private sectors. In this way, a department or company can create a sustainable organization that is able to focus on its key objectives, achieve them, and constantly learn how to improve itself.

Diane Lavoie, as a recently appointed head of an enforcement group in the Fisheries department, has quickly to diagnose the strengths and weaknesses of her organization and its capacity to meet its mission. She will have to understand and maybe even interpret the mandate she has been given. She will have to provide direction to her group in a way that mobilizes them to do the job. She will have to clearly define how her group will deal with clients, which in this case is more complicated because the ultimate objective is to protect the fish from being overharvested.

As part of government, she will undoubtedly face challenges with support systems, which may include materials, such as cars, boats, or computers, or staffing actions. She may even come face to face with the challenges of dealing with poor performance. Finally, a key to success for Diane will be to continuously learn what works and to develop a team that has the capacity to learn. In addressing all of these dimensions of productive organizations, Diane can build a strong team that is able to serve the department well.

Given the complexity of organizations and their tendency to be shaped by various coalitions of interests pursuing different objectives, or responding to events in a different manner, high performance attributes may not be easy to achieve—especially on a continuing basis.

1.5 Management Challenges in Modern Organizations

The challenges that managers face at any given level in order to achieve productive and effective organizations are considerable. This course is focused on the core challenges that first-time managers and supervisors face in a wide variety of organizations. The course includes a variety of cases involving government departments at the regional level, a central agency position, and a corporate service function. The course also includes cases on non-profits. Over time, other cases will be added to increase variety and to focus further on the first two levels of management. The aim of the cases is to put students in the shoes of managers and, through the experience of analyzing and discussing cases, to develop key insights into the choices that managers can make in a variety of organizations and circumstances.

The major textbook that was originally used for this course was John Kotter's *Power and Influence.* Unfortunately, that book is now out of print, but this course contains key readings from that source. This Guidebook will briefly describe the overall approach that Kotter developed to assess management challenges. These insights were developed largely through his study of general managers of corporations (J. Kotter, *The General Managers*) but his initial work was done on his study on mayors of large cities and their roles. Interestingly, he found that the key elements for being effective as a manager in either type of organization were very similar.

Kotter's insights are at the heart of this course. He argues that there is an irreversible trend in business and government toward increasing organizational diversity and interdependence (Kotter, *Power and Influence*, pp.12–51).

Diversity can generate extensive conflicts between individuals and groups with different perspectives or stakes in an organization and make it very difficult for managers to achieve a particular agenda or direction. Interdependence—when two or more parties have power over each other and require each other to get the job done—is also a growing feature of modern organizations. In organizations that are interdependent, unilateral action is rarely possible and co-operation is essential.

In diverse and interdependent organizations, the challenge for managers is to reconcile many different interests, conflicts, and priorities and bring them into a co-operative working relationship. Hence, management and leadership can be viewed as the "politics" of establishing the required coalition to achieve the aims of the organization or of implementing the manager's agenda.

Thus, the central theme of the "The Politics of Management" is the challenge faced by managers of modern organizations highlighted by their dependency on many players over whom they have limited or no authority, or who may have substantially different agendas or priorities. This can create what Kotter calls a power gap — that is, the difference between the amount of power needed to get the job done and the amount of power that the manager has.

For this reason, a session in this course is directly focused on improving the ability of students to assess the levers of power that a manager can use in a particular situation to overcome the inherent power gaps in a job.

Another course priority is to discuss how managers can develop an agenda that is implementable in the context of the growing power gaps that characterize modern organizations. To be successful in these situations, managers have to understand their organizational environment, the multiple dependency relationships they face, and the key opportunities and constraints that shape decisions. Out of this assessment, they must design an agenda, or strategy, that will maximize the chance of success and contribute to an effective organization.

Kotter argues that the most effective managers are those who develop an agenda, build a network, and implement their agenda through the network. He came to this conclusion through extensive research and interviews with general managers of corporations and of mayors of cities in the USA (J. Kotter, *The General Managers*).

Managers who are trying to implement an agenda or achieve a high-performance organization must bridge power gaps through the development of influence and co-operation with superiors, colleagues, subordinates, clients, and partners. In short, to be successful in modern organizations, leaders have to learn how to gain sufficient power and influence to do a job; and learn how to use their power and influence responsibly.

The challenges that Kotter outlines for managing organizations today apply to a wide variety of complex organizations. Similarly, the kind of assessment and analysis required to develop effective managerial strategies are remarkably consistent throughout government, business, and non-profit organizations.

The reason why Kotter's *Power and Influence* is such a useful book for studying management in the public sector is that government is the extreme version of a complex organization with high interdependence and multiple dependency relations. Moreover, the techniques that Kotter advocates for dealing with complex organizations today are highly applicable to public-sector organizations.

This "Politics of Management Course" has been designed to build a strong repertoire of analytical skills and the capacity to assess the management challenges for producing effective organizations and developing strategies that can apply to a wide range and types of organizations.

The next section of this Guidebook outlines the framework that the author has developed for the assessment of the management environment and the analysis of the choices and opportunities available to a manager. This framework is the centrepiece of the course and is utilized to analyze the cases throughout the course.

Thinking Like a Manager: A Framework

2.0 The Framework

The framework outlined in this Guide is the centrepiece for the "Politics of Management: Thinking Like a Manager" course. It was developed by the author in the early 1990s and was based on a combination of the approach outlined by Kotter (*Power and Influence*), and by Rosemary Stewart (*Choices for the Manager*).

The "Thinking Like a Manager" framework below deliberately places the manager in the centre of relationships with superiors, subordinates, clients, and other groups. It includes key concepts necessary for analyzing the relationship of the manager with these key groups and developing an agenda. "You cannot take the manager out of management" is one of the central premises of the course.

This is the course in one chart or framework. Students achieve the most learning by continuously applying this framework throughout the course to discuss management challenges and then applying the framework to management cases. The feedback from many students over the years is that the framework is the most useful part of the course because it gives them a way to make sense of complex management situations and then determine approaches or strategies for dealing with them.

The challenge faced by many managers is bringing together the people, resources, decisions, and key forces within the organization required to achieve a particular agenda or aim. It is critical that the manager align the key players and factors shaping the organization with the overall agenda. Executives must also recognize when constraints are real and when they can be overcome. They must, as Rosemary Stewart has shown, learn what kinds of choices they can make in terms of their role, the domain they will focus on, and their roles with respect to others.

The concept of alignment is key to understanding how managers can get their jobs done within the diversity and interdependency that characterize modern organizations. The key to managing an agenda successfully in most complex organizations, public or private, is to align all the factors that relate to the job—people, priorities, resources—so they mutually support and reinforce a particular direction. Then, over time, managers must keep adjusting, changing, and developing the key elements of the organization, the agenda, and other factors.

The "Thinking Like a Manager Framework" re-emphasizes the core focus of this course: the manager and the job. At the centre of the diagram is the manager, who must achieve an agenda and get a job done while dealing with superiors, subordinates, clients, and colleagues, as well as taking into account the external environment and the organization. The manager typically interacts with all of these areas simultaneously.

The manager is not just a person in a position. The manager is someone with a background, a reputation, and a certain set of skills. The managers must design their approach to the job based on the relationships they have and the requirements of the job, but also must consider their own credibility, skills, and potential to achieve a particular course of action.

In pursuing an agenda, managers are faced with issues, demands, constraints, choices, crises, personnel problems, conflicting priorities, and multiple objectives, cultures, and personalities.

The challenges that managers face are simultaneously short-term (a few minutes or hours) and long-term (several years). The issues range from specific and operational (e.g., who comes to a meeting, what should be done about a specific problem) to fundamental strategic issues of policy, organization, and service

CHART 1: THINKING LIKE A MANAGER FRAMEWORK

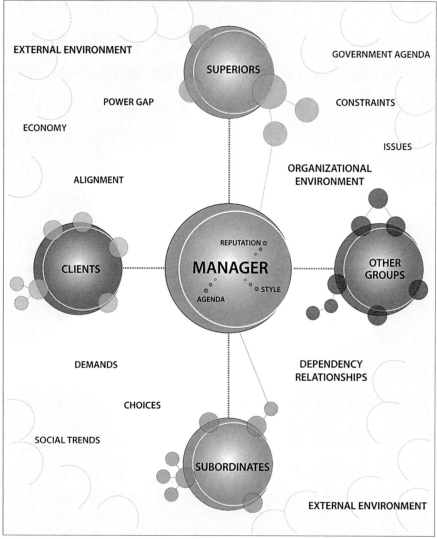

EXTERNAL ENVIRONMENT

GOVERNMENT AGENDA

SUPERIORS

POWER GAP

CONSTRAINTS

ECONOMY

ISSUES

ALIGNMENT

ORGANIZATIONAL
ENVIRONMENT

REPUTATION

CLIENTS

MANAGER

OTHER
GROUPS

STYLE

AGENDA

DEMANDS

DEPENDENCY
RELATIONSHIPS

CHOICES

SOCIAL TRENDS

SUBORDINATES

EXTERNAL ENVIRONMENT

© RICHARD PATON
The Politics of Management: Thinking Like a Manager

delivery, which could affect the organization for years. Managers must operate on all of these levels at the same time to be able to lead and direct the organization. A key challenge is to determine what needs to be done and where to focus among a myriad of possibilities.

The framework that will be used in this course is based on seven key elements that affect how managers manage. These include:

- Manager and the job

- External environment

- Organizational environment

- Relations of the manager with superiors

- Relations of the manager with subordinates

- Lateral relations of the manager with key individuals and groups

- Relationship of the manager and organization with clients

The better aligned these factors are, the more likely that a manager will overcome the challenges of diversity and interdependence and achieve a particular agenda.

Over the twenty years that I have used this framework, students have found that it provides them with an approach and concepts to make sense of what seems to be a complicated, confusing set of forces and relationships with no clear path forward.

In this course, students will learn how to use this framework to analyze the relationships between the manager and each of the elements. This will help students to improve their potential to develop strategies that can address various management challenges.

2.1 The Manager and the Job

The Manager

At the centre of this framework is the manager who has a particular agenda, or is in the process of developing one. A large part of how a manager deals with the agenda, or management issues, is the manager himself/herself.

It is essential to understand the manager and his/her style of leading an organization and the key strategies that the manager relies on to manage. There are some key references that can help students to understand these aspects of management. Students may refer to Stephen Covey, *Principle-Centered Management*, and Warren G. Bennis and Burt Nanus, *Leaders: The Strategies for Taking Charge*. Peter Senge in *The Fifth Discipline* discusses the leader as architect of a learning organization. In addition, the Myers-Briggs framework for identifying clusters of characteristics (extroverted, introverted, etc.) is useful for a manager to understand his/her own strengths.

Important aspects of management style include how the manager goes about setting the vision and direction of an organization and mobilizing people to carry out that vision. It is also vital to understand how much personal credibility the manager, or leader, enjoys in an organization.

Understanding the manager and his/her credibility and style are so important that this is the subject of Part III of this Guide, which focuses on the choices managers can make concerning their operating styles.

The Job

The second major aspect of the framework is the job for which the manager is responsible. The nature of the work, the accountability structure, the authority, and the resources available are important to understanding how the manager must act to achieve expectations.

To understand a management job, it is necessary to know the accountability requirements associated with the job. Osbaldeston's

Keeping Deputy Ministers Accountable provides some insights into the complex accountability requirements of deputy ministers and some of the differences between the public and private sectors.

Rosemary Stewart's *Choices for the Manager* is useful for understanding how managers define their jobs. Ms. Stewart relies on three very useful concepts for analyzing a management situation:

- Constraints: those factors that limit a manager in getting the work done

- Demands: those factors absolutely required to do the job

- Choices: the kinds of decisions managers make regarding their style, role, domain, boundaries, etc., while doing their jobs

It is also very important to understand the authority and the levers, in terms of decision-making, that come with the job.

Roles

What are the key roles that the manager must play in this job? Change agent, controller, resource allocator, or downsizer?

Is the manager focusing on relationships outside the organization, or mainly concerned with internal management?

Some questions vis-à-vis the manager and the job:

What are the key demands (absolute musts) on the manager at this point in time? Who is making these demands?

- Can the key demands or pressures be divided into long-term, medium-term, and short-term priorities, and managed as such?

- For the immediate demands, how long does the manager have to show real progress in addressing these demands?

- Is this particular manager oriented to developing positive working relationships with colleagues, superiors, and subordinates?

- What choices does the manager take with respect to defining his or her role (leader, negotiator, decision-maker, comptroller, firefighter, technical expert)?

- How well does this manager understand his/her own management style, its impact on others, and how to learn from experiences? (Refer to Chris Argyris, "Teaching Smart People How to Learn," *Harvard Business Review*, May–June, 1991)

- Is the manager able to establish trust with subordinates and communicate a vision that can generate commitment and support?

- What is the manager's style in gathering information and making decisions (open, consultative, closed, secretive)?

- How does the manager deal with superiors? Does the manager work on developing a common agenda with superiors, or try to keep them out of the way long enough to get his/her job done?

- What are the personal assets that the manager brings to the job that enhance his/her personal influence? What are the particular attributes of the manager that reduce his/her effectiveness and influence?

- How does the manager spend his/her time? How does this relate to organizational needs? Is it possible for the manager to balance new and existing demands on his/her time to achieve a particular agenda without a significant change in his/her approach?

The challenge is to figure out how to manage in a specific organizational context. Managers usually develop strategies that are contingent on the situation, but that also reflect their specific style and personal attributes.

2.2 The External Environment

An organization's external environment is critical to shaping the pressures on a manager. This external environment includes all those players or forces that are outside the direct chain of command in the organization. Generally, the role of an executive is to balance the demands and requirements of the external environment with the needs and requirements of the organization. If there is a significant change in the forces that make up the environment of an organization, the executive has to find a way to realign with those influences and manage the interface between the organization and the environment.

The following questions are relevant in our analysis of the environment:

- Is the manager working in a complex or simple environment; a stable or unstable environment?

- Among an organization's key sponsors or clients, is there a consensus on the organization's aims, objectives, mission, or operations?

- In the external environment, what are the manager's most significant dependency relationships? Upon what are these dependency relationships based (e.g., technology, need for support, resources)?

- Are there major trends and forces in the environment that support, or detract from, the direction of the organization? Are these forces, or trends, gathering momentum or dissipating over time? Force-field analysis, which reviews the forces for and against a particular change, is useful for this kind of analysis.

These dimensions of the environment can impact significantly on the manager's role. For example, the environment's degree of stability and complexity will impact on how executives spend their time. Generally, the more complex and unstable an environment, the more necessary it is for managers to devote their efforts to maintaining the relationship between the organization and its environment and to devote time to boundary-spanning activities (James D. Thompson, *Organizations in Action*, pp. 66–82).

In stable and simple environments, managers can often devote more time to the organization's internal management and operations.

A critical aspect of management is to assess the key players, trends, and influences that are shaping the organization and to understand how these will affect the manager's superiors and job. A critical characteristic of effective managers is their ability to align their agendas and actions with the trends and influences present in the environment and to take advantage of them whenever possible.

2.3 Organizational Environment

A manager works within the context of an organizational structure and division of labour, as well as within the social system and culture that shape the organization. Thus, it is critical for the manager to understand how the organization works and makes decisions.

The type of organization and its environment can have a profound influence on the nature of the manager's job. For example, there is a huge difference between a large tax collection organization, such as Canada Revenue Agency, and an agency such as Aboriginal Affairs and Northern Development Canada, which, as a federal department, is involved in a wide range of programs and services (e.g., housing, education, social services, and infrastructure) aimed at thousands of Aboriginal communities. The same differences exist in the private sector between large manufacturers, small retail organizations, and conglomerates with multiple product lines.

The evolution of the organization, its history, and the key events that have shaped its progress are important in understanding some of the elements of the manager's job. It is particularly important to understand the culture of the organization, the kind of people who work there, and how they view their mission.

The overall structure and the key information processes are also important to understanding the organization. If it is a large machine bureaucracy—a term commonly used by Mintzberg—it will tend to apply rules and hierarchy in making decisions. A different approach would be taken by a professional organization where high standards dictate the primary decision-making method.

Moreover, decision-making processes will be affected by the extent to which an organization has a high vertical or horizontal differentiation (i.e., different and distinct groupings or divisions of labour). The more levels and differentiation that exist, the more coordinating and integrating mechanisms will be necessary to implement an organization's essential functions.

As Kotter illustrates in *Organizational Dynamics*, organizations are constantly faced with the challenge of maintaining equilibrium among factors such as dominant coalition, external environment, technology, social system, hierarchy, and assets. These factors can shape the organizational environment and how the manager must respond to various issues and challenges.

A number of excellent references provide an insight into the analysis of organizations, for example, Harry Levinson, *Organizational Diagnosis*; and Henry Mintzberg, *The Structure of Organizations*.

Some questions on the organizational environment: These are important questions for managers to understand when determining what kind of priorities to pursue and how to pursue them.

- How does the organization generally respond to changes in the environment (responsive; rigid; head-in-the-sand; reactive; crisis-driven)?

- Does the organization tend to work as a unit, or is it highly balkanized and differentiated—with each unit pursuing its own goals—and with few unifying or integrating processes such as plans, human resource rotations, or team approaches present during decision-making? (See differentiation and integration concepts in Appendix A on concepts.)

- Do executives support each other to achieve overall goals or directions?

- How strong is the tradition of leadership by the deputy minister, CEO, or board of directors?

- Are there significant conflicts within the organization with respect to direction and mission, divisions of labour, or social systems?

- What are the core technologies, or work processes, present in the organization, and how do they shape its behaviour?

- How does the system of incentives and rewards function, and what kind of work is most valued?

2.4 Superiors

The relationship between a manager and his/her boss or bosses is a vital aspect of successful management. One of the most popular articles for students of the Politics of Management course is the article by J. Gabarro and J. Kotter, "Managing your Boss," which is included in the bibliography.

As Gabarro and Kotter point out, the manager has considerable responsibility for developing a positive working relationship with his/her superiors by understanding their agenda, working style, and requirements. This is straightforward and obvious, but it is amazing how many managers neglect this aspect of their jobs.

One of the realities of modern management is that managers may have more than one boss. It is increasingly necessary to consider a group of people as your superiors. For example, in a government department, an assistant deputy minister's superiors might include a deputy minister, an associate deputy minister, and a senior ADM. Sometimes the relationships with ministers and their staff can further complicate these superior-subordinate relationships and the accountability structure.

With the adoption of matrix organizations and functional reporting relationships, the same complexity might exist in the private sector. In the world of global corporations, the director responsible for a plant in Canada may report to several different global groups for different aspects of the business. For example, the plant director might have two or three different products and report to global business leaders for those products. In addition, the large global companies have a central public affairs function and the director in Canada will report to them on key policy and regulatory issues— especially those of a global nature like climate change.

Some questions on managing relations with superiors:

- What are your boss's or bosses' agenda and priorities?

- What pressures or expectations is your boss facing and how does this situation affect the way he or she does the job?

- When does your boss want you to deliver on his or her key priorities?

- How does your boss learn and make decisions?

- What does the boss expect of you as manager (what are his/her key demands)? How can the manager best help the boss achieve his or her agenda?

- What are the strengths of your boss or bosses and how can they help you achieve your priorities as a manager?

- What is your boss's style of management? Are there major conflicts or differences with your approach? How can you deal with them?

- If your boss faces stiff opposition from a stakeholder group or staff, will he/she continue to support the priorities and directions established by the manager, or will he/she retreat quickly at the first sign of resistance?

Never underestimate the importance of managing the relationship with superiors. Being responsive to your superiors is not only responsible management; it is a necessity if you want to get the job done.

The surprise for many students of the course when discussing this article is that managers and staff have to devote time and energy to managing their bosses, and that a subordinate can actually shape that relationship. Some students have actually tried some different practices as a result of this session in the course and found that they were able to change the dynamics of their boss-subordinate relationship by, for example, recognizing that the boss either liked or did not like detailed briefings; by determining how the superior liked to be informed; etc.

Given the diversity and interdependence present in most modern organizations and the difficulty in achieving results, your boss is a critical asset. Without her/his support, your power and influence are considerably diminished. Managers must find ways to augment their influence and reduce their power gaps by working in partnership with their superiors. When a superior's approach to management is incompatible with that of a manager's, or is inappropriate for responding to the organization's needs, there will be huge barriers to progress.

2.5 Staff

To achieve their own agenda, managers must mobilize their staff, on which they are highly dependent. Even though managers have direct authority over staff, they must rely on the same leadership and management techniques that are appropriate in dealing with those outside the chain of command, namely influence, as opposed to authority.

The degree to which the staff are committed to the manager's agenda depends on whether the staff

- Believe the manager is credible and can achieve the agenda

- Share a common vision on the challenges facing the organization and the path forward

- Get personal meaning from the leader's approach to the organization

- Participate in the creation of the agenda

- Believe the agenda will help staff develop their own skills and career

- Feel they will be rewarded in objective or subjective terms for helping to achieve the agenda.

To mobilize staff, managers must assess their own strengths and weaknesses, as well as those of the organization and staff. Managers must understand the limitations of authority and how dependent they are on staff to get the job done.

Managers have to determine what roles they can best play and where other people in the organization can contribute. Rosemary Stewart calls this work-sharing. By determining how to share work with key subordinates, managers, colleagues, and even people outside the organization, a manager can increase the time available to pursue other items on their agenda.

To be effective in dealing with change, modern organizations require managers who are creative; and open, positive and innovative environments where staff can challenge old assumptions but are still able to work as a team committed to the organization.

Some questions on managing relationships with staff:

- What are the demands placed on the manager and their relationships with their superiors? What is the impact of the operational style of the manager? For example, a manager working for a workaholic micro-manager will inevitably be affected by the situation and will have difficulty following a delegating style of management.

- Has the manager provided an agenda, vision, or purpose that can mobilize the commitment, trust, and support of staff?

- Is the organization for which the manager is responsible able to accomplish the agenda?

- What are the work demands, incentives, constraints, and factors that affect how staff do their jobs?

- Are there key people in the organization who will be able to facilitate or inhibit the achievement of the agenda, or the demands the manager is facing?

- Are there major organizational, management, personnel problems, or constraints that must be resolved?

- What are the expectations of staff with respect to leadership style, participation, vision, and approach to decision-making?

2.6 Key Individuals and Groups

All organizations have key groups on whom the manager is dependent and that can be mobilized to help achieve her/his agenda. The distinguishing factor among these groups is that, unlike staff, the manager has no direct authority over them.

It is essential to identify such people and groups and to understand their perspectives and agendas. As Kotter has suggested, to achieve their agendas, managers must build the required network of individuals and groups, both inside and outside the organization, and then implement their agenda through the network.

It is often useful to analyze the dependency relationships between executives, certain groups, and other key players to determine the extent to which they have power over your management agenda. Then, it is important to determine their degree of support. By understanding the degree of power others have over your agenda and their degree of support, one can quickly determine who is absolutely essential to the achievement of an agenda. If you cannot figure out how to get the key players to support your agenda, you may have to find a different agenda.

There are some ways to develop these co-operative relationships; some of these are outlined in *Power and Influence*, chapter 4. In a typical organization, however, the key groups and individuals involved in a particular decision will vary tremendously according to the subject or issue at hand. For example, a manager may be extremely dependent on the vice-president of finance and vice-president of marketing to develop and introduce a new product. On the other hand, if a manager wanted to change the distribution of a product that has been successful for years, the dependency relationships would be very different.

Some questions on managing relationships with key groups and individuals:

- Who are the key groups and individuals on which you depend?

- What are the agendas, perspectives, and views of these key people, and what pressures are they facing in their jobs? What incentives affect their behaviour?

- How would you analyze these key groups and individuals or their degree of authority or influence, and your need for their support to achieve your agenda?

- What kinds of approaches could be used to build positive working relationships and partnerships with these key groups or individuals?

- What kinds of approaches could be used to neutralize or minimize the degree of harm they could do to a manager's strategy?

A manager who can develop creative approaches for building coalitions required by the organization is often highly valued and is able to accomplish tasks that others only dream of.

Clients

To a large extent, the purpose of an organization is to serve its clients. Whether the organization is serving fishermen, consumers, bank customers, or car buyers, clients are a key part of a manager's job.

Much of the literature on total quality management and the experience of some of the most successful corporations have focused on forging a positive relationship with clients. This is done by knowing what clients or customers want and knowing how to serve them, by constantly being sensitive to changes in needs or requirements and by measuring performance. The same approach can be used by governments when dealing with its citizens.

Some organizations have used the client as the focus for defining the manager's agenda and mobilizing the support of superiors, colleagues, and subordinates. Many corporations and government departments are also developing new organizational and management approaches by focusing on the client and the quality of services delivered.

Some questions on managing relationships with clients:

- Who are the organization's clients?

- Are there major conflicts between the needs of different clients?

- How do clients feel about the organization (from well-served to very irate)?

- How does the organization (superiors, subordinates, colleagues) deal with clients?

- In government organizations, it is important to know how powerful the clients are, as a group, and how they may influence policy decisions.

- How do superiors, subordinates, and colleagues work, as a whole, to meet and respond to client needs?

- What are some of the key impediments to serving clients better (management approach; systems; skills; distribution of functions; key people; etc.)?

- How does the organization measure client response or satisfaction and reward those who work to improve client satisfaction?

Managers who develop a strong and positive approach to dealing with the needs of clients can often increase their influence in an organization.

Unfortunately, in many organizations, a client-focused perspective is at odds with traditional practices. It often requires an energetic and focused leader to be able to make this kind of change. Focusing on clients can also be a useful tool for realigning other parts of the organization behind your agenda (changes to organizational structure, changes to technology, etc.)

Summary and Challenges
for Managers and Supervisors

We started this Guidebook with examples of three first-time managers in a policy group, an enforcement group in Fisheries, and a golf course.

In carrying out their jobs and developing an agenda, these managers can employ this framework to understand the challenges they face in their external and task environment, the agenda and style of their superiors, their dependency relationships with other groups and their agendas, and the capacity of staff.

For the new policy director, this will provide an essential understanding of the organizational context within which he or she works and the areas that should be assigned the highest priority. Using the concepts of the course, these new managers will be able to assess the demands, constraints, and options they face and make important choices. Moreover, they will be able to identify the most important functions they must adopt and the choices they can make with respect to their domain. Likewise, they will know how to manage boundaries with other organizations and staff.

If these first-time managers follow the advice of Chester Barnard and focus on the job of maintaining the organization—setting direction, ensuring commitment of staff to the goals of the organization, and managing the interface of the organization with the environment—they will develop a stronger understanding of their role as managers and provide essential value to the organization.

As Linda Hill has found out in her research, managers essentially learn by doing. By combining an active interest in assessing their jobs and situation with hands-on experience, managers can adjust to their jobs more quickly and learn how to be effective in creating a high-performance organization.

Through this process and assessment, these new managers and supervisors can overcome some of the challenges faced by first-time managers, as identified by Linda Hill, in defining their role and establishing their managerial identity.

Understanding the Operating Style of Managers

3.0 Overview

Since the manager is at the heart of the framework for the "Politics of Management: Thinking Like a Manager" course, it is important that this Guidebook provide some insights into the choices that managers can make that define their managerial identity.

The "Thinking Like a Manager Framework" that has been designed for The Politics of Management course places the manager at the centre of a set of complex relationships and issues. There is absolutely no doubt that a manager can make a huge difference to the success or failure of an organization, and that leadership and/or operating styles vary enormously among managers.

Over the years, the most perplexing challenge that many students of the Politics of Management course have faced is figuring out how to work with their boss.

In the discussion sessions in the course, students have identified the full range of managers: micro-managers, who don't trust staff to do anything; absentee managers, who seem to be disconnected from the organization; and power-seeking managers, who enjoy divide-and-conquer tactics with the staff, or taking over the territory of other groups.

The most common observation by students is that their managers are changing so quickly and the styles can be so different that they are constantly figuring out how to work in a changing environment. The second most frequent observation is that the managers seem unprepared for their jobs, and often are in survival mode and uncomfortable in the management role.

On the other side of the coin, students, either through working in government and non-profits or through co-ops, have identified excellent managers. They are successful because they know how to work with staff, superiors, and colleagues in developing an agenda and mobilizing staff to co-operate in achieving the main objectives. Unfortunately, for every ten students that describe their experiences working with managers, only about two will identify really exceptional managers who are comfortable in their jobs.

This section is aimed at helping students analyze the leadership or operating style of a manager so that students can, first, understand the manager they are working with; and second, learn how to work in the most productive way with that manager.

The section draws from the literature in this area, but also relies on the insights of the author in his thirty years of experience as a senior executive in government and head of a business association.

3.1 The Operating Style of Managers: Four Choices

The management or operating style of managers is usually defined by the way they define their role and organize themselves to do their jobs. This is reflected in the degree of control they seek; how they balance work, family, and personal interests; the trust they have in others; how they build teams; and their personal sense of competence.

To be able to manage successfully, new managers must develop an operating style that takes into account their strengths, work-life balance, the way they make decisions, work with teams, and their overall approach to the organization.

There are four key decisions that managers will tend to make as they develop what Linda Hill called their "managerial identity." These are outlined below with some of my personal insights from various management roles.

Most managers adopt an operating style early in their careers and stick to it—even when it is sometimes inappropriate to the situation.

This section will provide some insights that will help in the assessment of management and operating style. It also aims to integrate the thinking of key authors who will help students understand the depth of literature that is involved in this field.

This section covers four choices that determine management and operating style:

- How managers choose to adapt their style and role to the situation they face

- How they balance work, family, and health and ensure renewal

- How they define their role as a manager and leader of a management team

- How they structure organizations and decision-making in relation to their management approach

All of these choices will have a cumulative impact on the organization's culture and its performance.

In management, there are many variations of management or operating styles, and one can be an effective executive with many different types of approaches. However, managers can make some critical mistakes that usually mean their success over the medium or long term will be seriously compromised.

3.2 Choice 1: Choosing the Manager's Role

The situation and expectations that a manager faces in an organization can vary tremendously. Some of the factors that can shape your management style are:

- The nature of the organization itself (Canada Revenue Agency is much different from Aboriginal Affairs and Northern Development Canada; a computer company like Apple or RIM is much different than a petroleum company like Exxon Mobil)

- The superiors you report to and their management style

- The team that is in place when you assume responsibility for the organization

- The culture and history or identity of the organization

- The issues the organization faces (no major issues on the agenda vs. a crisis affecting the department or government)

John Kotter has an excellent example in his book *Power and Influence* of an executive who was given a week to turn around an organization that was going bankrupt: He called an emergency meeting and at the first sign of serious resistance to developing a turnaround plan, he fired two executives. Although the approach he took might have been completely inconsistent with his normal operating style, it was what he had to do in the situation. His dramatic decision got the group to understand how serious it was, and that he was clearly in charge. Notwithstanding the very poor odds of success, he mobilized the team to develop a turnaround strategy and he accomplished his objective. This was the kind of approach he needed to take in a time-sensitive, emergency situation.

Management styles can be very incompatible. If you are an executive who tends to lead organizations through clear priorities and high delegation, your management style will be severely constrained by a micro-manager who focuses on issues and expects you to know everything about every file. If you stay in the job, your approach will have to adapt to this situation or it will take a personal toll on you.

Every job and organization has its history and culture. If the last executive was liked, respected, and effective, it is very important to recognize that a dramatic change in style will not be welcomed by the organization. In this situation, it is smart to find out what worked and build on it. If changes are needed, they should be made carefully and gradually.

If the culture of the organization is generally viewed as functional, and is strongly oriented to regions of the country or services, an executive will have to respect this and show that he or she is part of that culture. Without the credibility of being part of the organization, the executive will have difficulty getting the support needed to do the job.

Staff that are used to lots of communication, participation, and delegation will not respond well to a micro-manager who is secretive. On the other hand, an organization that is used to a strong leader might react negatively to a leader who constantly consults everyone and is slow in making decisions. The reality is that any incoming executive is compared to a predecessor — either positively or negatively.

Finally, an aspect of the situation that you face as a manager is your personal life. If you are recently married with young children, your time pressures at home will be quite different than those of an executive who is three or four years from retirement with grown-up children.

One of your decisions regarding management style is how you want to balance your work and personal life. Do you want to protect your family-work balance? Do you want to pursue other interests? Do you want to ensure enough time for exercise, sports, and health?

Executive coaches encourage managers to think these

questions through when determining their approach to their jobs. All too often, managers let the work define their priorities completely, and wonder why their families are strangers or why their marriages disintegrate.

Following are examples of different situations and challenges that a manager can face and that can affect their style:

Change agent

The manager was recruited as a change agent. He/she is expected to change the organization better to reflect the mission of the department, or the views of a minister or senior executive.

Turnaround executive

The manager is more than a change agent. He or she is expected to reverse a major financial or program problem by whatever means necessary. This situation assumes the organization is failing; if personnel, organizational, or financial decisions are necessary, the turnaround executive's biggest mistake is to be too timid in making them.

Consolidator or continuous improvement facilitator

In this situation, the organization has already been convulsed by change, or perhaps had an executive who created serious turbulence in the organization. The role of the manager is to bring some order, stability, and calm to the organization and restore it to its basic operational effectiveness.

Issue manager

In some instances, there are only a few issues the top executives of the organization care about or need to address. In this instance, the manager's job is to deliver results on these key issues and—as long as the organization is functional—this is all that is expected.

The management situations are not always clear, and the role of a manager is to figure out those expectations. Even though there will be some impact on the role and style of a manager in different situations, the best approach is not often clear. These are the areas where a manager has to fully assess the situation and have the depth and maturity to review his/her management style and determine how best to approach it.

A manager who is expected to deliver a stable organization and focus on a few issues—but is determined to act like a turn-around executive—will run into huge problems with superiors and colleagues. Similarly, a manager who aims to maintain the status quo with minor improvements, when the key leaders want a change agent and a turnaround, will not be fulfilling his/her responsibilities.

The most difficult management situations are when there are a number of mixed signals—turnaround, change, maintain continuity, and manage a few issues, etc.—combined with different demands by superiors or key colleagues. Moreover, these expectations may change over time.

In this case, the manager must determine what are the expectations, or even help his superiors and others decide what the expectations should be. This consultation will need to include superiors and subordinates as well as key outside groups.

Summary

It is imperative that a manager assess the total environment he/she faces and the choices they will need to make in their approach to the job. Moreover, their chosen path should be aligned with the needs of the organization, the styles of their superiors, and the history and culture of the organization.

3.3 Choice 2:
Choosing How to Balance Work and Family and Other Interests

Most executive coaches find that one of the major problems facing leaders of organizations is to find the right balance between the demands of the job and their family, personal interests, and health.

Many managers have had abbreviated careers because they were not able to find this balance and as a result ended up as what Richard Boyatzis and Annie McKee call a "dissonant leader." These authors illustrate in their book *Resonant Leadership* that executives can create a pattern of behaviour as a result of stress that eventually becomes self-defeating in terms of effective leadership, personal health, and family.

Many studies in the federal government and some of the work by Linda Duxbury at Carleton University in Ottawa have revealed high stress levels among public service managers and staff. These stress levels can result in amazing patterns of behaviour that show up in outbursts and cycles of what Boyatzis and McKee call the "sacrifice syndrome." This syndrome relates to a pattern whereby the manager determines that only he or she can do the job and takes on all the responsibility. He or she works harder and harder and makes little progress; relations with superiors and subordinates deteriorate.

Given the demographic challenges that many organizations face today, it is very likely that many government and non-profit organizations will have executives in key positions who are simply not ready for these jobs. Regardless of the growth of executive coaching, it is likely that many supervisors will not have the support mechanisms in place to get good advice or to help subordinates achieve the necessary balance to remain effective.

One of the hallmarks of the executive coaching field is to advise executives to make clear choices early on in their jobs regarding time allocation, balance of work and family, and health or renewal. Stephen R. Covey calls this putting time aside for "sharpening the saw," or keeping yourself mentally agile, physically healthy, and balanced.

Personal insights

If you work in organizations for any length of time, you will find that there is tremendous variation in how managers balance work, family, and outside interests. Some executives willingly sacrifice their health and family for work and pursue career advancement relentlessly. This tendency is often unrelated to the requirements of the job; it is related to the values and interests of the manager.

In contrast, some executives create clear limits on work in order to have a quality family life, preserve their health, or simply recharge. One example of this was a deputy secretary in the Treasury Board.

In a fairly work-obsessed environment, a new deputy secretary in a central agency announced his priorities when he started the job. He announced that family-work balance was a top priority, and that he was going home to his family no later than 6:30 p.m. Any briefing notes or letters after that time would not be dealt with until the next day. (Fortunately, Blackberries were not yet in use at that time.) He also communicated that he would leave any evening event he attended at 8:30 p.m. at the latest. He was always available to put his children to bed. These signals also helped other staffers who were trying hard to balance work and family in an organization that put a premium on working at all hours and had scant regard for family life.

Second, he made it clear that he wanted a number two person in the organization to whom he would always delegate tasks while on holidays—and when on holidays, he would be unreachable. Many other executives rotated this responsibility and, in effect, did not have a delegated number two. In high-pressure jobs where you absolutely need time to recharge, this is really important. This arrangement always gave him the comfort that the job would get done in his absence and also that he was developing another executive. Both designated acting executives eventually earned major promotions—one to senior ADM and one to deputy minister.

A major problem for managers is that their health deteriorates on the job and they do not devote enough time to renewing themselves. Their families also suffer, and the rate of separation and divorce is high. This deterioration of the body and family relationships will affect not only their physical health but their emotional health and capacity to lead organizations.

Summary

There are far too many managers, with huge potential, who ignore the need for balance and renewal. The worst offenders are those who think they can continue to work excessive hours and take on more and more responsibilities without this affecting their competence and effectiveness as leaders. Eventually, it will. The worst of the worst managers expect staff to do the same.

It is also imperative that executives make clear choices about how they will spend their time in a job and the balance of work, family, exercise, etc., to ensure continuing renewal.

3.4 Choice 3: Choosing your Role as Leader of the Organization and Management Team

In any job, it is important to reflect on your character and approach to people in the organization. At the core of management style is character, personality, and trust.

There are many different tests available to determine your dominant traits as an individual. The Myers Briggs assessments are very good for showing whether you are E (extroverted) vs. I (introverted]); an (N)intuitive (big thinker and future-oriented) vs. (S) sensor (step-by-step, incremental); whether you are a thinking type of personality (T), or inclined to relate to people's feelings (F), and whether you tend to judge (J) (make decisions), or (P) perceive (tend to wait and see, and have extensive discussions).

A good reference on Myers-Briggs is *Type Talk: The 16 Personality Types that Determine How We Live, Love and Work*, by Otto Kroeger and Janet M. Thuesen (1988). This book illustrates how the various combinations of personality attributes affect behaviour in the work environment and elsewhere. In the course, one class will be devoted to the question of leadership style and will include the Meyers-Briggs framework.

One renowned author on the importance of personality and character for management is Stephen R. Covey. He has written a profound book, *Principle-Centered Leadership*, which explores the values and principles that guide managers and their relationships. Covey's work has spawned a major management consulting enterprise that provides workshops to corporate clients.

The character of a person affects their management/operating style.

As Covey writes:

> An emotionally immature person will tend to borrow strength from position, size, strength, intellect or emotions to make up for character imbalance. This builds weakness in the manager, weakness in others (who react with conformity or limit their own creativity) and weakness in relationships because fear will replace co-operation, defensive patterns of behavior emerge that stifle innovation and open sharing of information or debate. (p. 83)

Covey also illustrates that when managers are able to establish a set of consistent principles that are understood by the organization combined with trust, a highly empowered organization can be created. However, he clearly illustrates that the core requirement for this is the ability of the manager to trust others and create interpersonal relationships. "You cannot have empowerment without first having trust." (Covey, p. 65)

An organization managed by a leader who is insecure, who does not trust others, who is self-serving, and who has arbitrary opportunistic principles will ultimately create a culture that breeds fear, second-guessing, over-control, and under-commitment of staff.

Core character and principles of managers

The core character and personality of a manager is a major contributor to management and operating style. Thus, a big part of developing a management style is self-awareness of strengths, weaknesses, and tendencies. Effective managers will use this awareness to guard against their weaknesses and build on their strengths. They will build a team that complements them, as opposed to mimicking them.

What role can executives choose as leaders of the organization or leader of the management team? Following Covey, these choices will depend on the character and competence of the leaders and their trust of others or capacities in terms of interpersonal relations.

The basic choice managers have about their roles in a job are as:

1. The Boss. They view themselves as "in charge of the organization," "the boss," with separate groups or even individuals reporting to them with the need for considerable direction and guidance.

2. The Team Leader. They view themselves as the head of a team that is responsible collectively for managing an organization and the relationships with superiors and other groups.

The team leader sees his or her job as working with the team to make key decisions affecting the organization, and when necessary the leader will make the final decision. The team leader recognizes the need to use the talents of the group to challenge each other and work together on policy, program, financial, and personnel decisions.

In at least three major management jobs, this author has had to create a management committee because his predecessor did not have management meetings and took all the decisions himself. In each of these cases, the author even faced resistance to attend such meetings on the basis that it was not "their" job to worry about the overall management the group. When each of these organizations faced major challenges, the ability of the management group to work together was critical to success. If you are a committed team manager, sometimes you might have to work to develop the team.

Covey has illustrated that when managers operate with a clear set of principles that are understood by staff, empowerment can occur. This enables staff to take the initiative and innovate, knowing the principles that the manager will use in decision-making.

> If you focus on principles, you empower everyone who
> understands those principles to act without constant
> monitoring, evaluating, correcting or controlling. Prin-
> ciples have universal application. And when they are
> internalized into habits, they empower people to create a
> wide variety of practices to deal with different situations.
> (p. 98)

Many executives who follow this approach build on sports analo-
gies such as a hockey, basketball, or football team, where success
is the result of teamwork and everyone doing their jobs—but
working with each other. There is no doubt that personal experience in sports teams heavily influences those executives.

One of the most interesting recent books on management
is *Good to Great* by Jim Collins. This book describes empirical
research on eleven companies that made the transition from good
companies to great companies in their particular sector.

There are a lot of amazing insights in this book, but the three
most important ones relate to how successful CEOs recruited
their management team; and their particular management style.

With respect to choosing the management team, Collins was
surprised to find that there was a major difference between the
way good companies and great companies recruited their management team. The great companies did not follow the usual practice
of selecting the best people for particular jobs or to implement the
organization's strategy. They went for the absolute best people in
their business and then found a spot for them in the company—
even if it was not a perfect fit. (p. 63)

Once the team was established, it was expected to come up
with the strategy. This approach is exactly what Wayne Gretzky
did to create the winning gold medal team in Salt Lake City. He
was quoted as saying: "I want the absolute best players, and
then we will decide what roles they can play. I can turn a skilled
scorer into a checker but not the reverse." Canada won! Gretzky
reversed the trend of Canada's producing good Olympic teams
but not great ones.

The second observation was on leadership style. Collins identifies what he calls Level 5 leadership in all the leaders of the great companies. He found that Level 5 leaders "embody a paradoxical mix of personal humility and professional will. They are ambitious to be sure, but ambitious first and foremost for the company, not themselves."(p. 39)

Level 5 leaders display a "compelling modesty, are self-effacing and understated." In contrast, "two-thirds of the comparison companies (i.e., ones that did not transition to great) had leaders with gargantuan personal egos who contributed to the demise or continued mediocrity of the company. Level 5 leaders are fanatically driven, infected with an incurable need to produce sustained results. They attribute success to factors other than themselves. When things go poorly, however, they look in the mirror and blame themselves, taking full responsibility." (p. 39)

Another publication that provides loads of insights into management or operating style is *Managing for Excellence* by David L. Bradford and Allan R. Cohen. These authors make a distinction between a "heroic manager" and a "manager as developer," which is very useful.

The attributes of heroism that Bradford and Cohen argue are not suited to contemporary management challenges are as follows:

- The good manager knows at all times what is going on in the department.

- The good manager should have more technical expertise than any subordinate.

- The good manager should be able to solve any problems that come up.

- The good manager should be the primary (if not the only) person responsible for how the department is working. (pp. 10–11)

They argue that this "heroic" approach to management results in a lowered quality of decisions and the tendency to withhold information from the top executive, because the executive is not encouraging and welcoming others to be part of the problem-solving. There is an attitude that develops in these organizations along the lines of "he or she is the boss and I just do what I am expected to do." Or, "Around here, the boss wants to make all the decisions, so I just send the information to him or her and wait to see what happens."

In an organization led by a heroic manager, the top executive tends to take on more and more responsibility (assuming others cannot do the job or that he/she must do it), resulting in a self-defeating cycle where subordinates pass more and more decisions to the top executive, and subordinates take on less and less responsibility and are less and less motivated by their jobs.

> The manager is driven to get more involved—to be as central to the department as a nerve center or orchestra conductor—desperately trying to control all the diverse parts of the organization, but still unable to produce excellence. (p.17)

Bradford and Cohen argue that managers in contemporary interdependent and changing organizations must "tap the energies and potential of talented subordinates whose skills and knowledge are vital for dealing with complexity and change." (p. 21)

They promote a "manager as developer" model, where the top executive works with a team in a framework of shared responsibility to assess the needs of an organization and set goals for improvement. This approach creates a higher commitment to excellence, feelings of responsibility of staff, and higher motivation. (pp. 62–75)

An important talent that the manager brings to the table is to be able to create the environment where the best possible ideas and decisions come from the group discussions, and the synthesis of various perspectives and experience.

An effective manager can continuously make a team function far better than its individual parts and create a sense of collective responsibility and ownership for the success of the organization.

Ineffectual managers, regardless of the situation and needs of the organization, take on all the responsibility for the organization, depriving their managers of the potential to be responsible for the organization's success. They drain energy from a management team and end up with the lowest-common-denominator decision or one that depends entirely on the thinking of one person.

These are some important decisions that managers must make in determining their roles and style in leading the organization: staffing, teamwork, empowerment and trust, and communications.

Staffing

Whom you staff as your executive assistant or secretary is critical to the organization. This role reflects you. All managers with any office experience have faced assistants who are guard dogs, protecting their boss, wielding power over staff, and creating an atmosphere of hostility. At the other extreme, an executive assistant who is very respectful of others, personable, and helpful will constantly create a positive atmosphere and a sense of co-operation and teamwork in an organization.

Teamwork

An executive who sets the tone constantly that he or she expects people to work together, to learn from each other, and use their abilities to come forward with the best solutions will eventually obtain that result. This can be done by positive reinforcement but also by indicating clearly that backbiting, unwarranted criticism of colleagues, and bureaucratic games are just not appreciated and certainly not rewarded.

Empowerment and Trust

Fear is one of the most toxic aspects of an organization. An executive who creates an atmosphere where staff are empowered and do not fear to make a mistake will be rewarded with an innovative organization. An executive who inherently trusts people to work hard and expects them to achieve their best will usually find that is what happens. An executive who jumps all over his staff — criticizing them before understanding the situation completely — can erode the morale of an organization very quickly.

One CEO that this author worked with told a story that illustrates this point. He was a scientist working in government doing experiments. One morning, he came in at ten a.m., and his boss chastised him for being late and did not even ask for an explanation. Actually, the scientist was in the middle of a time-sensitive experiment where he had to come in from two a.m. to four a.m. to measure the results. He was dedicated to his job and to the results of the experiment. The scientist told me: "That is when I decided I could no longer work in that organization." After that, he never even bothered telling his boss why he was late.

Communications

Probably one of the most important factors is how the executive communicates with staff. Does he or she communicate only with direct supervisors in a hierarchical system? Is there communication throughout the organization of the challenges and priorities to ensure all the staff are aware of the expectations and goals? Are there opportunities to ensure that information and advice flow from all parts of the organization when dealing with issues? Do the personnel collaborate across functions and work with others outside the organization in a positive and constructive way?

All these decisions affecting the role of managers and how they staff, communicate, and create teamwork in the organization are vital aspects of management and operational style.

A critical choice for a manager is to define early in their tenure the role they will play, their priorities, and how they will work with the management team and overall staff. Some executives actually introduce themselves to an organization by clearly outlining how they like to work with their management group and describe some of the main elements of their operating style.

These managers are usually those who have developed the self-awareness necessary to be able to understand how they impact others and the ways to be most effective as leaders of an organization.

3.5 Choice 4: Choosing How to Structure the Organization and Decision-Making

Another key choice for an executive is to decide how to manage the structure of the organization and decision-making. As Covey notes, these decisions will also depend on the trust the manager has of others and how he wants to ensure the alignment of the organization.

With a strong principle-centred organization, and good staff, the structure can be flat and flexible, with open communication. With an executive who mistrusts others, there will be a tendency to hierarchy and control or elaborate processes to limit the discretion of staff reporting to the manager.

No matter what your operating style, a manager of an organization is going to have to respond to the priorities of his superiors and clients. His or her style will be affected by the operating style of the head executive.

The way executives make decisions is also a critical element of operating style. Often this aspect of operating style can be understood only by observation or past practice. The decision-making approach will also reflect the executive's views and trust of people and their capacities in terms of interpersonal relationships.

Some executives will choose to invest in group decision-making about the priorities and direction of the organization. They will ensure that this direction has the strong support of superiors and subordinates and is in alignment with the needs of clients and the organization's culture.

The opposite extreme involves an executive who likes to manage every issue and be involved directly in all the administrative and financial decisions of the organization. A great way to understand this is to find out the signing authorities in the organization: Who has to authorize a contract or staffing action; or approve travel. Another is how the executive reviews briefings and the requirements for sign-off on the less important files.

Some executives will never take the officer with the most knowledge of the issue to meetings with superiors. Others regard it as essential to provide development opportunities for staff and to provide the best possible information for decision-making. One director that the author reported to early in his career noticed that briefing notes did not have the name of the officer who prepared them on the document. He quickly changed that to make sure his bosses knew who was directly responsible for the file. All these are indications of the degree of control an executive wants on the transactions in the organization and relationships with superiors.

These varying approaches to decision-making are often reflected in the approaches executives take to organizations. Organizations can be designed so that decision-making is extremely hierarchical and continuously depends on "top-down," detailed direction, or they can be designed to be much more collaborative and innovative information-sharing groups.

There is a huge variation among executives in how they organize work. This will depend a lot on whether they are heroic managers or managers as developers.

The reorganizers

Some executives reorganize every time they change jobs. These organizational changes are usually premised on some lofty goal or change in priorities. Typical war cries for organization are: "We need to break down the fiefdoms and stovepipes"; "We need to realign or re-engineer our processes"; "We need to reposition our organization to achieve our new strategic priorities."

In many cases, these organizational changes are driven more by the need of the executive to put his/her stamp on the organization, establish control, or recruit executives who fit their particular operating style or whom they trust. These executives also tend to bring a band of loyal followers with them because they cannot trust the staff who work in the organization; or they need the comfort of familiar faces that are completely dependent on them for their careers.

Some executives like to de-layer any organization they move into so they can get as many people reporting to them as possible. They do not like having to be dependent on a few executives who run "their" organizations. There are many cases of absolute recklessness by executives in reorganizations that undermine morale and create serious problems for years.

Executives, especially those without the ability to sense the mood or feelings in an organization, can totally underestimate the impact on people in terms of uncertainty, morale, and the sheer complexity of reclassifying and staffing jobs. My personal observation is that executives who are inclined to make major organizational changes on a continuing basis are usually high in Thinking (T) and Judging (J) categories in Myers-Briggs and high on the Intuitive ranking (N). Conversely, they are usually low in the Feeling (F) category.

In many of these organizational change situations, the entire department is aware that the organizational structure will not last long after the executive leaves. In many cases, it is well known that the change in organization has little to do with the effectiveness of the program or department.

In Covey's words, these managers are not service-oriented (i.e., thinking of the organization's clients or its staff). They are driven to change for self-interest or to ensure that the organization conforms better to their operating style; or they have a highly conceptual idea of structure and decision-making, whether it is functional or not.

Some leaders are notorious for reorganizing. It is their modus operandi when they are appointed to a department. Staff check with the department formerly managed by this leader and quickly hear: "Watch out! He [or she] will reorganize the place in the next few months or de-layer the organization, and it will never be the same." When you see this train wreck coming down the track, find another job.

The program managers

On the other hand, some executives approach organizational change very carefully. Their focus is on delivering the results of programs, and some actually start with an operating assumption that you should not change the organization for the first year on the job.

Their motto is: understand how it works first and then see if change is needed. This fits well with John J. Gabarro's work on managers who take charge of organizations. (See *The Dynamics of Taking Charge.*) Gabarro observed that after an initial "taking hold" stage where some immediate and necessary changes are made, most successful executives go into what he calls an immersion stage, where they get to know the organization and determine where improvements can be made. The major changes come about eighteen months into the job when they know exactly what levers to pull and what changes to make.

Unfortunately, in government, eighteen months is a very long time. Ministers, deputy ministers, and many other levels of management often do not stay in their positions for that long. Gabarro's research is still very useful because it is likely that managers have to go through the same stages in taking charge of an organization, but probably act faster in government, and to a lesser extent in non-profit organizations.

Others do not view structure as that important unless there is a huge obstacle in mandate or capacity. Their view is that it is the people who really matter. Hire the right people, and they will figure out a way to achieve the aims of the organization. In general, this group of managers is wiser, less egocentric, and accomplishes more than the "reorganizers."

The reluctant reorganizer

Finally, there are also reluctant reorganizers. This group starts with the premise that reorganization should only be done when absolutely necessary for major strategic changes in the business of the company or department.

They are painfully aware of the impact that reorganization can have on morale and the stability of the organization. They are also very conscious of the challenges of rewriting job descriptions, classifying new positions, recruiting new people, and the toll that a reorganization can have on productivity. On a Myers-Briggs type indicator test, they would probably show up with a better balance between Feeling (F) and Thinking (T) because they view an organization through the perceptions and feelings of others, as opposed to simply viewing it as structures and boxes or ideas.

In government, a reorganization often takes two years to implement, including approvals and the staffing and classifying of new jobs. In one reorganization in a federal department, the director of one group was still acting after three years because the job had not been classified and staffed on a permanent basis. It is not unusual to find a situation where another reorganization is starting when the last one has not been totally completed in terms of classification and staffing—resulting in constant churning and uncertainty for staff.

The reluctant reorganizer finds that in order to achieve a change in organizational direction, or to change the management team, the only way to do it is to change the organization. This type of executive also makes the organizational changes that are absolutely necessary and tries to create, through the change, an almost immediate gain in terms of organizational coherence and morale. He/she manages the change very carefully, with sensitivity to impacts on people. This kind of executive can make an organizational change a win-win for most participants and does not create the kind of destruction that reorganizers are known for.

In addition to organizational structure, principle-centred leaders will choose organizations that enable highly motivated people to innovate and achieve the directions of the organization, whereas heroic or control-oriented managers will seek organizational structures that reflect their personalities or needs, as opposed to those of the organization or staff, and provide ways to limit the authority or flexibility of staff.

Personal insights

The author has been the architect of four major organizational changes: three in the Treasury Board of Canada Secretariat and one in the Office of the Auditor General. I have also been subjected to what I would call random violence in organizational changes when I was a young policy analyst at Indian Affairs.

In all of these organizational changes, I probably would be called a reluctant reorganizer, but in every case, the decisions that were made related to strategic changes in the functions of the group.

The organizational changes were sometimes the result of government-wide decisions, such as the elimination of the Office of the Comptroller General, resulting in the integration of the Audit and Evaluation group with the Administrative Policy Branch; or the elimination of the Ministry of Privatization and Regulatory Affairs when Regulatory Affairs became part of the Administrative Policy Branch at Treasury Board. In these cases, the challenge was to integrate new organizations into an existing organization.

My observation on reorganizations in government, after observing dozens of them, is that most are poorly thought-out and ineffective. They do not deal with the fundamental requirements for organizational success, are driven far too much by the egos of senior executives, and are implemented exceptionally poorly. This leaves staff confused, uncertain, and demotivated. Few reorganizations produce a net gain in performance for the organization.

The best example I can think of is a department that had a deputy minister who was notorious for reorganizing, based on an esoteric and very personal model of decision-making. He created elaborate processes and matrix groups where reporting relationships were unclear and responsibilities even less so, reduced to: "Do what the DM wants."

Everyone in government and industry knew that the DM's reorganization would not last a month after he left. And when he left, far earlier than he expected or wanted, it became clear to his successor that the organization could not work. When asked whom she reported to, one director in the spaghetti-like organization said: "I have no idea. I report to a room." The DM had made a choice. He may have rationalized that the organizational design was related to the needs of the organization, but it was far more related to his unique operating style of decision-making.

Summary

A key indicator of the management style is how the executive makes decisions or how the organization makes decisions. Who is involved? How are they involved? Does the executive ensure the key information and perspectives are part of the decision?

Does the manager look for and encourage alternative views and recognize his or her biases or weaknesses in making decisions, as well as strengths?

The approach to organization can be related directly to the character, competence, and personality of the lead executive. The approach managers take to organizations will sometimes vary according to the situation they face, but will also be determined to a significant degree by their personalities and approach to working with their teams.

Successful executives learn to design organizations to meet the results of the department or business and refrain from elaborate changes that are simply an extension of their personal preferences or ambitions. They also focus on changes that will last well past their tenure as executives.

Conclusions:
The impact of management and operational style on the organizational environment

These choices on management and operating style can have a major impact on the working environment of an organization.

A manager can create a hostile, risk-averse, fear-ridden organization with micromanagement and mediocrity in performance. Or another manager can create an innovative, respectful, team-oriented and service-oriented organization where people love their work and feel they are making a contribution.

Anyone who has worked in an organization and witnessed a change of CEOs, DMs or ADMs, DGs, or other managers has been surprised at just how much difference a manager can make to the atmosphere of an organization. This is one of the first lessons that a young person learns in an organization.

Organizational performance studies show that innovative and productive organizations are associated with a positive working environment that encourages innovation and focuses on results and teamwork. When surveys of these quality organizations are carried out, they provide a 360-degree feedback on the operating style of managers. Many of the questions in these surveys relate to the degree of openness, trust, and communication in the organization and the extent to which staff feel they understand objectives and directions and are participants in the organizational decision-making.

These choices for a manager on operating style will determine how managers spend their time, how they work with a management team and make decisions, and how they work on the substantive issues facing the organization. All of the choices will determine the overall organizational environment and ultimately the performance of the organization.

3.6 Lessons for Students of the Politics of Management Course

One of the most important lessons that young professionals need to learn early in their careers is to understand themselves and their tendencies in terms of management and operational style and to work on improving their ability to lead organizations in positive ways.

Linda Hill's book *Becoming a Manager* has an excellent chapter on the "transformation" required for becoming a manager. She notes that "managers must act as managers before they really understand what their job is or what they are supposed to do" (p. 231). This insight leads her to conclude that managers learn best by a constant interaction between experiencing the job and its requirements along with the development of their abilities in terms of interpersonal judgment, self-knowledge, and the ability to cope with stress and emotion (see p. 230). In her view, managers need to be "highly proficient at learning from experience in an organizational context" (p. 239).

Earlier in this Guidebook, a few examples were used of first-time managers taking over a policy group of sixteen people or a manager becoming responsible for an enforcement group in a fisheries department. As new managers, these individuals should not only develop the capacity to understand their environment, dependency relationships, and power gaps; they have to make serious choices about their operational style.

Is Jacob Martin as the new head of Policy in Aboriginal Affairs going to continue to be the lead person on a particular policy file that he had before becoming director? How will the manager set priorities and manage the overall team? All of the four key choices identified in this section that govern operating style will be relevant. As a new manager, many of the choices will come quickly. The question is whether Jacob, with his limited experience as a manager, will recognize these choices and consciously make decisions about his approach to management.

Diane Lavoie, as chief of Enforcement, and Ron Storie will also face challenges determining what role they should play in their group, how they will work with their team, and how the organization and decision-making should be structured. All three will be much better off making these decisions if they have good role models, some basic understanding of the operational style that will work best, and the approach that is best suited to them. Unfortunately, like many first-time managers and supervisors, they will probably end up learning on the job.

Another important lesson for first-time managers and supervisors is to recognize that all management positions involve "power stress." Managers have to find ways to maintain a balance between work and family, protect their health, and ensure continuous personal renewal.

These choices provide a framework for discussing management challenges and for gaining further insights into the operating style of managers described in the management cases in the Politics of Management course.

In reviewing readings and discussing cases or management issues and challenges, ask yourself:

- What kind of management style does this executive have?

- What is driving the executives' approach to their jobs and the way they work with their management teams and others?

- Does this management style fit the situation and will it contribute to the overall success and effectiveness of the organization?

- How could the executive improve his/her overall management and operating style?

Also, if you are managing a group or ever expect to be a manager:

- What kind of management and decision-making style are you likely to have?

- What are the areas where you are likely to be strong as a manager, and where you need to improve?

The answers to these questions will help you to understand your own operating style as well as others and hopefully understand how the interaction of these operating styles is likely to work.

SECTION IV

Management Strategies and Skills

4.0 Overview

This section pulls together some of the major management strategies that are relevant in the Politics of Management course. This section has been added to this Guide because it brings together some of the strategies that emerge in the class discussion with respect to specific management challenges or cases. Obviously, this is not aimed to provide an exhaustive list of potential strategies. Section IV aims to provide some insights into the kinds of strategies that can work and those bound to be failures.

4.1 General Guidance on Management Strategies

Kotter in his research found that general managers of private organizations are successful when they undertake the following:

1. Develop an agenda, taking full account of their environment (superiors and other groups), as well as the organization

2. Develop a network to achieve their agenda

3. Implement the agenda through the network

To be able to achieve this involves not only the development of managerial skills; it also requires an ability to "think like a manager."

Management is the practice of getting the work of the organization done through people, and managers must be able to develop a vision or an agenda and establish the required strategy, organization, support, and resources.

There are many approaches or strategies that managers can employ to achieve their agendas. Some are outlined in detail by Kotter (*Power and Influence*); others are depicted in colourful detail by Gordon Chase and Elizabeth C. Reveal (*How to Manage in the Public Sector*). The book by Chase and Reveal is based on the experience of Gordon Chase as an assistant secretary in Washington, D.C., and a department head in the city of New York.

There is an art to developing an agenda. The manager must be able to assess the total picture: external environment; superiors; subordinates; key groups and clients; trends; specific issues; demands. Then, the manager must pick a direction and course of action that achieves synergy, or alignment, among the key elements required to carry out the job. Each element of the framework can complement the other to produce an increased probability of success. Each of these aspects of the job may act as amplifiers that together can generate enough power to obtain the broad spectrum of support necessary for implementation.

A manager who has a very clear agenda and a strong management team ready to implement it—but no support from superiors—has a problem.

Alternatively, a manager who has agreement on priorities with senior management, but does not have the staff or organizational capacity to accomplish the agenda also has a problem. In these cases, the manager will ultimately have to change the agenda, the staff, or the organization.

Finally, an organization where everyone is working co-operatively to achieve a common agenda that is, in turn, not aligned with the needs of clients, faces a major adjustment by the key players. Just think of the many corporations that have floundered with products that did not fit the market, or client needs, even though enthusiastically supported by the total organization.

To overcome the power gaps inherent in diverse and interdependent organizations, managers must have many skills. They must be able to establish an agenda that can be implemented and is capable of motivating staff and include a vision that can gain the support of other key groups. The following must be undertaken:

- Understanding people, their characters, their agendas, and the organizations where they work

- Understanding the substance of the work for which the organization is responsible and how best to do the work

- Developing extensive co-operation and support from superiors, subordinates, colleagues, and clients

- Making hard decisions about what can be done now, rather than later

- Developing a strategy or sequence of actions whereby one success can build on another; and gradually the manager is able to make major changes because of the base of support that has been put in place

- Making a careful self-assessment of personal strengths, weaknesses, operating style, and suitability for meeting the challenges ahead

- Making decisions about who can help them get the job done and who would want to see them fail

- Developing organizations that can improve continually and are capable of learning from experience

- Making judgments about people, the work being done, and when to initiate a change

- Adopting solid principles upon which people can depend and that can guide decisions on a daily basis

- Making hard decisions on the capabilities of staff as part of the team required to achieve the agenda

Managerial skills include an ability to assess a total management situation (authority relationships, organizational context, people, timing, political issues, degree of choice, etc.). It requires a capacity to act and implement an approach to the development and strengthening of the organization. This course of action is often based on a combination of experiences, judgment, analysis, intuition, and personality.

It would not be an exaggeration to say that management does involve some "street smarts" about people and power. Sometimes organizations can get really nasty and managers must have to have the ability to recognize this when it occurs. This is not a job for the naïve. Some of the best deputy ministers I have seen have an incredible ability to assess people relationships and events in the decision-making process and then position themselves to have maximum influence at precisely the right time.

The critical requirement for a course of action to succeed is a strong alignment between the agenda and all of the key aspects of the manager's job and the operating style of the manager. An ambitious agenda involving a great deal of change will require considerable support from superiors, key groups, and staff. Without this, the agenda will be a "bridge too far." A more focused agenda concentrating on only one or two minor operational changes will not require nearly the amount of external support and changes in staff.

If managers neglect one or two key elements of this framework, they will usually find that their agenda falters due to opposition from a key group or area. This is why Kotter and this course put so much emphasis on the concept of power gap. Where there are significant power gaps, managers who do not find a way to overcome these gaps will falter in achieving their agenda.

4.2 Six Key Management Skills

In addition to the framework for "Thinking Like a Manager," the course will focus on the development of six key management skills.

1. Analyzing the External and Organizational Environment

To "think like a manager," it is necessary that students understand the trends, forces, cultures, and interests that are either working for, or against, a particular manager; and how to identify the approach that will maximize support in the environment and within the organization. A key here is to find the point of maximum support for a given direction, or the point where others will not bother to oppose it. This is what could be called the "zone of consensus," where there is sufficient overlap in the trends, or interests, of key groups for a course of action.

2. Diagnosis of Organizations

To "think like a manager," there is a need to analyze organizations to determine the major strengths and weaknesses that enhance or limit their potential to achieve a high level of performance. This could include leadership issues, culture, systems, technology or processes, or any other key area that prevents or limits the organization from achieving its full potential. There is a wealth of literature that can increase the managers' strength in analyzing organizations.

3. Assessing Power Relationships

A key skill in "thinking like a manager" involves the analysis and assessment of who, in or outside your organization, has the power that can make a difference to your agenda. Whose support do you need and what will it take to move them from being negative to being neutral or positive?

4. Understanding Management Styles

Managers need to develop self-knowledge or the ability to understand how management style, personality, ways of thinking, approaches to decision-making, and interpersonal relations can affect managerial success. Without this skill, it is very difficult to assess their own potential to develop and implement a strategy.

5. Establishing an Agenda

Managers need to develop an agenda or strategy in a complex situation. The agenda defines what the manager should do. Picking the right set of priorities is often difficult in complex management situations and can lead to many fruitless initiatives.

Developing an agenda is more than picking a few priorities or setting a few objectives. It requires a combination of analysis and perspective combined with some intuition and street smarts. It requires an ability to see the whole pattern and then choose an approach that is workable.

When developing an agenda, you have to estimate the overall dynamics of decision-making that Kingdon outlined earlier in this Course Guidebook, assess the potential for support, and recognize how to develop the required alignment among key players and trends to be successful. This is a learned skill and takes time and experience to develop.

One of the best ways to learn how to develop an agenda is to observe how experienced and wise managers develop an agenda. In some instances, the creativity involved in assessing the best approach in a very complex situation is simply amazing. By observing this, aspiring managers can be inspired to think creatively in the face of seemingly insurmountable challenges.

6. Implementing an Agenda

This skill requires the ability to link all of the key elements required to successfully implement an agenda. This includes an understanding of the key supporter required, the nature of the organization, the systems needed, and the challenges of implementing programs.

In the public sector, the implementation of programs is a particularly difficult challenge, because it involves the delivery of services to citizens in the context of government regulations and numerous political factors. Often, policies and programs are developed in government without sufficient consideration of implementation realities.

To counter this, a good technique to use is "backward mapping." Instead of starting with the policy change and neglecting some of the important implementation realities, backward mapping starts at the interface of the policy or changed program with the client. Then, the manager works backwards to determine what is necessary to make the policy change work. This could involve staff, computer systems, co-operation with other governments or organizations, etc. In government, implementation is often 80 percent of the job but gets about 10 percent of the effort in the initial policy development.

Since management involves getting work done through others and requires communication concerning the purpose and approach to a given challenge, implementation is a constant challenge. It requires constant reinforcement of direction and adjustment, when required. Since it takes a huge effort to get all the key groups aligned to achieve a particular direction, a major mistake in implementation is to give mixed signals concerning the agenda or direction.

Throughout the course, these six skill areas will be developed through readings, cases, and studies of managers or guest speakers. To help students to reflect on their skills in these areas, the exercise below can be completed.

Exercise

Students should use this page to assess, on a scale of one to ten, the six skills outlined in this section with a one-sentence explanation. Explain how you can further develop these skills through your work and educational experiences.

1. Analyzing the External and Organizational Environment

2. Diagnosing the Organization

3. Assessing Power Relationships

4. Understanding Management Styles

5. Establishing an Agenda

6. Implementing an Agenda

4.3 Death Moves

One of the favourite phrases for students of the course is what I call "*death moves.*" This concept is borrowed from a famous golf instructor, Jim McLean, who illustrates that there are many variations in a golf swing that can work, but there are some moves that are so bad they make it impossible to hit the ball well consistently.

There are "death moves" in management. For example, there are moves or decisions that essentially undermine your credibility as a manager, aggravate an already difficult power gap, or create an unworkable agenda. In addition, a "death move" can be a decision, or the absence of a decision, to deal with an issue that is absolutely necessary to resolve to achieve the agenda. They include the following:

1. Overestimating power and adding to power gaps

2. Timidity in achieving agenda when given carte blanche or a major challenge

3. Failing to change or challenge a major constraint

4. Failing to develop a working relationship with a superior and failing to build on the superior's power

5. Over-promising and under-delivering

1. Overestimating power and adding to power gap

Organizations are littered with examples of managers who could not achieve their agendas. In most cases, this was because the managers set out an agenda, or promised results, only to find out later that they did not have sufficient support of senior management; or that they were dependent on a key group or even staff that would not co-operate. In fact, some managers develop an agenda, or course of action, and then proceed to alienate the very groups that they depend on to achieve the agenda.

As a general principle, the most effective managers develop an agenda and network that you know you have the power and support to implement—even if it means keeping your agenda modest and developing it in stages.

One deputy minister in the federal government who had a strong tendency to come up with creative, bold agendas did not account for the fact that his vision and persuasiveness were not enough to overcome the reality that departments and business groups had their own agendas. Also his agenda was always associated with an increase in the power of his department over others—a death move in itself. The result was a bold initiative that stumbled along, faltered, and then failed. This did not help with his credibility, and he eventually left the government.

2. Timidity in achieving the agenda when given carte blanche or a major challenge

Occasionally, a manager will be asked to be a turnaround, or change agent, and is given a clear mandate to make the change. For entrepreneurial and ambitious managers, this can be a dream come true, and they will utilize every ounce of support they can muster and take full advantage of any flexibilities required.

The "death move" is to play it safe. When superiors make a demand that involves a major change and tell you they will exercise their power to support you, you in fact have a rare surplus of power for achieving an agenda. If you do not take full advantage of it, your credibility as a manager will decline accordingly.

This can be a particular challenge for first-time managers. Without a lot of management experience, one can easily become very cautious about implementing a bold agenda. When a major change is involved, there is also likely to be serious resistance. Notwithstanding this challenge, if the expectation is to be a change agent, the manager must build the agenda and team to achieve this, or his or her credibility will be diminished.

The same dynamic can occur if you are faced with major pressure to change a budget or program. If you do not recognize the seriousness of the issue and get ahead of the issue, your precious credibility will be reduced. At this point, superiors and possibly clients will recognize that there is a gap between what is needed and what the manager is able to accomplish—eventually resulting in questions about the manager's suitability for the job.

A good example of this in the world of non-profits is dealing with budgets. If the governing board is uncomfortable with a growing budget or fee increases, the president must maintain sufficient credibility to chart a course of action. If the president of an association does not recognize this and come up with a realistic and frugal plan, the association, and particularly the president, will face a clear power gap.

One would then hear comments like this from the directors of a board:

"We told him/her we had concerns about the budget, but he could not re-examine what the association is doing and find ways to streamline."

"We are not sure we can trust the president to manage the organization efficiently and make the hard choices necessary, so we will have to make them."

If you get to this point, as a manager in a non-profit organization, you are in big trouble: your commitment, credibility, and trust are compromised. In one organization where the executive director made a big pitch to expand the budget and the fees at precisely the wrong time, his spending discretion was removed by the executive committee to the point where he was executive director in name only and subsequently lost his job.

In contrast to the "death moves" described above, a manager can face a serious financial challenge and respond with a creative plan that addresses the issue and responds to the concerns of the board. He/she can also set the table so that the organization can review the options and explore the value proposition of the organization for members. By taking this approach, managers can often increase their credibility and strength as the leader of an organization.

3. Failing to change or challenge a major constraint (e.g., personnel)

Another "death move" is deeply rooted in the personalities of managers and their operating style. Some managers when confronted by a rule or a constraint quickly give up and "fold," saying:

"Oh, I cannot do anything about that. The personnel department claims I have to follow this process."

"I would like to hire that person but I don't have the budget or flexibility."

"I understand that the program would be far more client friendly if we made a change, but my hands are tied by departmental policy and our computer system."

When constraints, rules, or roles of central agencies, etc., seriously affect the feasibility of achieving an agenda, a manager has to be willing to challenge the status quo and create flexibility.

The acceptance of constraints is a major "death move" if you are expected to be a change agent or turnaround leader and if you allow unnecessary obstacles to thwart your ability to renew or improve an organization.

This is a particular challenge for first-time managers who might not be familiar with the staffing, classification, information technology, or financial system of an organization. For that reason, one important aspect of taking on management responsibilities is to understand the dependency on these groups, their constraints and agendas, and find ways to achieve an agenda in this context.

Stewart (*Choices for the Manager,* pp. 7–8) found out in her research on managers that there was a lot of variance between managers on how they perceived constraints.

Some viewed a constraint as immutable, and others just took it as a challenge to be overcome by asking the purpose of the rule or constraint, asking who was responsible for it, meeting the staff involved to see if there was a way to deal with the constraint, or inventing a new approach that avoided the constraint entirely.

This is not to say that some rules and processes do not need to be followed. Public servants must follow the law. Leaders of non-profit organizations need to follow the governance structure of the organization and policies of the board. Notwithstanding these realities, there are many perceived constraints in an organization that are not fixed in stone but still seem to pose major barriers to the effectiveness of a manager or organization.

Another dimension is the failure to negotiate expectations. For example, your boss asks you to write a very important briefing that he says he needs by Monday morning. It requires two days of work and the involvement of your staff. Some people would just work all weekend. They would demand staff do the same—only to find out that Monday was not a hard time frame after all.

Without creating an issue, managers can ask superiors and others if there is any flexibility in the date, or get clarification on how much is required by Monday, and how much later on. Surprisingly enough, many times there is much more flexibility than expected and the superior actually respects that a manager is trying to understand the exact requirements to carry out the job.

4. Failing to develop a working relationship with a superior and failing to build on the superior's power

Gabarro and Kotter (*Managing Your Boss*) outline the importance of determining how to work with your boss, an area where "death moves" are frequent. It argues that it is your responsibility to figure out how to work with your boss. This means figuring out how they like to get information; how they make decisions; their comfort level in terms of the manager's discretion and initiative; and so on.

A major "death move" is to fail to understand your boss and how best to work with that person. Some managers fail here because they just assume that bosses like to boss and that it is their responsibility alone to tell you what to do. This does not account for a boss who is a high delegator and expects you, as manager, to come forward with the ideas, and then he or she will make the decision. Some superiors will simply not respect you if you don't challenge them. They expect it. Others see such challenges as a "loyalty problem," and hence one needs to be careful in raising concerns about the decisions of superiors.

Some subordinates badly overestimate the amount of comfort the boss has in terms of information and may find that the boss is very unhappy because the subordinate does not provide regular updates on files. Whatever the tendencies, it is essential to understand the four types of choices outlined in Section III of this Guidebook. The simple fact is that there are huge differences in how superiors approach their jobs and how to work with them effectively.

Of all the possible "death moves," this one seems to be the most prevalent for first-time managers. As part of the transformation to a managerial role, it is critical to develop the capacity and flexibility to understand superiors and to work with them to forge a common agenda. This often requires some development and self-reflection, which is not common even among top executives.

Argyris (*Organizational Learning: A Theory of Action Perspective*) indicates that managers are exceptionally poor at understanding their own management style and its impact on an organization. His research on executives indicates that managers' stated approach to management, or their "*espoused theory in action*," can be different than their behaviour, or "*theory in use*." The former is the theory that a manager communicates to others; the latter is what he/she actually does (p. 11, above).

Argyris concludes that the only way to figure out how to work with one's superiors is to observe their behaviour and actions and, from that, derive their true management style. A classic example is the manager who says: "I have an open door policy" because that is what he thinks he should say, or actually believes it in theory. But if you observe him, you can see the assistant guarding the door, his schedule, and his very low interaction with staff. His actual "theory in use" is the opposite of what he claims.

One manager in a United Nations (UN) organization was exceptionally good at working with people of all races and backgrounds, but could not develop a good working relationship with his boss, the director general. In their meetings, the boss would consistently avoid making decisions.

The manager involved was highly efficient and usually knew exactly what decision had to be made and at what time. But in meetings, the director general would continue to create delays, forever increasing consultation and process requirements, and making it impossible for the manager to direct his staff and manage his programs.

One day, just by chance, the manager sent an email presenting several options and requesting a decision. Surprisingly, within a few hours, he had received a decision. Apparently, the boss could make decisions electronically far more easily than in person. By the way, President Richard Nixon was similar. He hated interpersonal conflict and preferred a written brief, where he would write nasty side comments and make a decision, much as he had done as a lawyer. Thus, the UN manager stopped trying to meet with his boss and when he wanted a decision, he sent an email. He had figured out how to work with his director general.

A major "death move" is to avoid doing the hard work of figuring out how your boss likes to work and make decisions and then adjusting to that style. The reality is that when there is synergy with a boss you have much more power to achieve your agenda.

5. Over-promising and under-delivering

There is a strategy that is exactly right for most managers: under-promising and over-delivering. Never put yourself in a situation where you consistently do the opposite by over-promising and under-delivering. Once that pattern has been established, your superiors, staff, colleagues, and clients will discount any initiative or agenda you present by assuming that anything you promise will not happen.

First-time managers are seldom aware of just how dependent they are on staff and other groups to achieve an agenda. Thus, they can easily assume that a particular job can be done without understanding the many constraints, dependency relationships, and difficulties they will face. Nevertheless, it is important to carefully assess these aspects of an agenda. A first-time manager who is able to do this for his or her first few challenges, and successfully implement an agenda, will develop a reputation for results. In most organizations, this usually translates into considerable power and influence beyond the specific levels of authority inherent in the job.

In most organizations, staff and colleagues are constantly making the assessment of whether a particular initiative is worth their time. A good deal of the assessment is the potential of the individual manager to deliver on a proposed agenda. They are assessing the managers' judgment and capacity to develop and implement an agenda. A manager with a strong track record of success will get the "benefit of the doubt," while others will have to prove themselves before others will commit to the agenda.

Summary

These five "death moves" are a small sample of the types of mistakes that managers can make, especially as first-time managers. There are many more "death moves" that could be described, but the main purpose of this section is to illustrate how easy it is to fall victim to a major mistake that can undermine a manager's credibility and effectiveness.

Managers should focus on all of the requirements to successfully implement an agenda. They should assess the organization, the dependency relationships, the agendas of superiors, and so on. In addition, it is useful to ask what could be the major "death moves" in a situation. Then, figure out a way to avoid them.

4.4 Three Cases of Middle Managers

This Guide started with three examples of managers struggling with their roles in the same way that Linda Hill discovered in her research.

Each of these cases illustrates the challenges faced by managers or supervisors with a question that will help focus students on the lessons of the course.

Diane Lavoie,
Chief of Enforcement, Maritime Region

After six months in the job, Diane is finding her role very difficult. Of the twelve enforcement officers she has reporting to her, three are perpetually facing serious conflicts with fisher groups to the point where they are sending letters to the minister and making press statements asking for their resignations. Diane has to figure out if this is the normal churn that occurs between enforcement staff and client groups, or whether these three individuals are just not able to work with fisher groups constructively. Moreover, one of the other enforcement officers has a drinking problem that has resulted in some safety issues for other staff.

Diane is facing another problem. She was just promoted to the job six months ago and already she is facing a new boss as regional director of the Maritime Regulatory Affairs function. She had an excellent working relationship with her previous boss and for that reason she had been promoted into the job.

The new director has a completely different management style, which could be called "command and control," where he issues orders, or directives, without much knowledge of the operational situation. The previous director understood the complexities of enforcement and always made sure that his decisions, or guidance, were aligned with the needs of the enforcement group to get the job done. Given that fisher groups are extremely knowledgeable of the rules and regulations, any slip-up by the department can create even more conflict and tension with clients.

Diane has already faced three examples where she had to explain and defend a director's decision that did not make sense—resulting in even more conflict with the fisher groups and calls for the resignations of the fisheries officers.

Although the director is very strong in dealing with administrative issues, such as the budget, and has the confidence of the regional director general, his style is creating havoc for Diane and her staff. Unfortunately, he is completely unaware of the impact he is having and does not seem open to reflecting on how his actions affect the enforcement unit. As a new chief of enforcement with little management experience, Diane is wondering how to work with her director.

Diane is also struggling with defining her role. As an enforcement officer, she worked on the boats surveying the fisher groups and met with these groups over allocations and catch limits. She loved this kind of interaction, and took pride in her ability to understand them and negotiate with them. In this job, she is constantly having to deal with correspondence from HQ and fisher groups, developing the budget, attending meetings with the director and director general, and coming up with ways to improve operations with less resources. She is not sure she is good at this, but she likes the challenge of organizing and managing a group so that it can achieve its mission.

Finally, Diane herself is starting to wonder if this job is worth it. She has two small children, and her husband has a good job in a government department. They live in a relatively low-cost maritime community, so their income is good for the area and the quality of life is excellent. She is now travelling more and more and spending at least two to three more hours each day at the office. In fact, she has to think about the job all the time— especially how to work with her new director and to deal with the staff.

Question: If you were a friend of Diane's and she asked you for advice, what suggestions would you give her that would help her to make the transition successfully to her role as chief of enforcement?

Jacob Martin: Policy Director

The policy group reports to a DG of Policy, Research, and Evaluation who, in turn, reports to the ADM, Policy in the Aboriginal Affairs department. The research group deals mainly with claims-based research support for lawyers and Native groups. The evaluation group is responsible for the evaluation of all programs in the department. In addition, there is a federal-provincial group dealing with issues that affect the federal relationships with the provincial governments. The four groups work well together and

the director general is superb at creating a positive and innovative work environment.

The domain of the policy group that Jacob is leading includes
a number of policy areas such as housing, self-government,
education, socio-economic development, and a number of rights
issues related to migratory birds and hunting, fishing, and trap-
ping. The group is also responsible for a unique project involving
an agreement with the Cree in Northern Quebec. Other than the
rights areas, there are operating programs in each of these areas
that are run by the ADM, Operations and the five regional directors general in the department.

The policy group is a constant hive of activity, and it is a
challenge to balance the various demands for policy development, along with the heavy correspondence on the rights issues.
However, in a few short months, Jacob has adapted to the job
by setting out high, medium, and low priorities for guiding the
work of the branch and has also streamlined some of the correspondence work to provide more flexibility for staff. He has also
strengthened relationships with his DG and the ADM and has
gained credibility as a good director.

One of the most urgent challenges that faces Jacob is the
development of a cabinet document on education. The government has a thin agenda regarding Aboriginals but believes this
is one of the few areas where they can make a difference. Previ-
ously, Jacob was the senior policy officer for education. Another
senior policy advisor replaced him in the education area when
Jacob was promoted to director. However, he is not as good
as Jacob in developing the cabinet document, and the clock is
ticking.

Jacob is struggling with the temptation to simply take over
the writing of the document during a week of seclusion, which
he is quite capable of doing. He knows that if he does not deliver
the cabinet document draft, he will lose some credibility and not
fulfill a key demand of his job.

He also knows that, as the policy director, he has to wean
himself off this kind of role. He has to provide sufficient direction
to get the cabinet document done, but not do it himself. There are

others in the group who are not as familiar with education policy but who are excellent at writing cabinet documents. In fact, the best person for this is working in the evaluation group and recently completed an evaluation of the education policy. Finally, there are a lot of issues surrounding the cabinet document that need guidance from senior management and other groups, such as corporate finance, Treasury Board, and some of the Aboriginal groups, especially staff that have been successful in developing educational institutions. To assist his group in developing the cabinet document, he must also work with these groups.

Question: If you were Jacob Martin, how would you define your role in managing this group and determine the best way to meet your priorities?

Ron Storie: *General Manager of Heritage Golf Course*

Ron Storie was sitting in his office in the clubhouse reflecting on how short a distance he had moved geographically—100 yards—and how much change he had experienced in his role and responsibilities. Instead of his office in the pro shop with the constant flow of members and phone ringing for tee-off times and merchandise, he was now surrounded by financial statements on the overall operation and a load of specific issues concerning the food and beverage service, as well as issues on machine purchases and leases for the maintenance of the course.

He was preparing for the next board meeting by getting acquainted with the golf club policies and procedures for the board. Fortunately, he did not have to be the secretary of the board because there was already someone, the assistant general manager, who knew how to prepare the agenda and provide guidance to the board on governance issues.

He also realized that one of the major influences in determining this approach to the job was that he did not want to follow in the footsteps of the previous general manager.

The former GM had been an incredible micromanager who was constantly directing the manager of the food and beverage department and the pro shop and, in many ways, undermining the morale of the staff. One of the reasons that Ron took this job was that his health simply could not cope with another GM like that. Given the past track record, there was better than a fifty-fifty chance that the next GM would not be competent.

By accepting the GM position himself, he figured that, at least in this way, he would be the boss. He did not want to end up managing like the previous GM, but he also did not want to end up losing his job like so many others before him. He was aware that there was an association for general managers, and several very successful general managers in his region. He was wondering if there might be any way he could tap into some advice on how to do this job. He also knew the president of the club very well, and she had been the main architect in the removal of the previous GM and in recruiting Ron for the job.

Ron was wondering what kind of discussion he should have with the president and other key players in the club, such as the club captain, other board members, etc., about the job.

Despite his business degree and training in golf club management at Georgian College, he recognized that he knew little about the management of the agronomy aspects of the golf course (the grounds, including fairways, greens, equipment, etc.) and he knew even less about the food and beverage operation. His assistant general manager was very knowledgeable about the administration of the club, such as membership, fees, financial management of accounts, and the operation of the board. As a professional golfer, he was quite respected for his ability to work with members, but he also had little experience working with the board— even though he knew all the board members as golfers.

One of the golf club members was an executive coach, and Ron was thinking of approaching him and asking him for advice on how to make the transition to the general manager's job.

Question: If you were asked by Ron to be his executive coach, what advice would you give him concerning his priorities and how to build a network for carrying out this job?

4.5 Executive Coaching: A Luxury or a Necessity?

When the author started to teach this course in the mid-1980s, executive coaching was virtually unheard of in the federal public service. In the past decade there have been major developments in this area. The federal government in Canada developed a coaching network through the leadership of Paul Lefebvre, who is now a very successful independent consultant in executive coaching.

Many corporations have developed coaching programs. Organizations such as New Ventures West have developed intense courses to provide accreditation for executive coaching. There are now standards for coaching accreditation recognized by professional bodies. It is surprising to see how many executives now utilize coaches to help them assess the challenges they are facing and improve their overall performance and perspective on their jobs.

The fact that executives are willing to pay hundreds of dollars an hour for advice reinforces the point that Kotter has made in his book *Power and Influence*: The challenges of leadership are far greater than the leadership capacities available to meet these challenges. Years ago, Kotter argued that more investment was required in developing programs to meet this leadership challenge. Executive coaching is one of the methods to bridge the gaps between the demand for leadership and the supply of effective leaders and managers.

What is Executive Coaching?

Mary Beth O'Neill, in *Executive Coaching with Backbone and Heart*, states that:

> The essence of executive coaching is helping leaders get unstuck from their dilemmas and assisting them to transfer their learning into results for the organization. (p. 5)

She explains that the coaching relationship is set within the context of a team and an organization. One of the key functions of coaches is to "build leaders' capacity to manage their own anxiety in tough situations."

One concept that O'Neill uses to explore the relations of an executive with his/her team and organization is the "social interactional field." This is the web of relationships among people. O'Neill describes this interactional field as something like a spiderweb that is strong but flexible. (p. 43)

When students in the Politics of Management course identify the key issues they face as young professionals, it is often exactly this network of relationships with managers, colleagues, and others that is the source of the most frustration. O'Neill places a lot of emphasis on learning to understand what she calls the interactional force field by observing how people react to a particular executive and how they react to each other (p. 45). This provides a rich source of information in coaching to determine a way forward that is more productive.

Another towering expert in the coaching field is James Flaherty, who founded New Ventures West, a coaching organization and network based in California. Flaherty uses an approach called "integral coaching," which focuses on understanding the whole person as part of the coaching process. In his book, *Coaching: Evoking Excellence in Others* (p. 27), Flaherty places major emphasis on a deep assessment of the individual before the coaching process can begin and the careful adaptation of the overall approach to coaching the individual client.

Flaherty uses several concepts that are powerful in the field of coaching. First, he makes an important distinction between an "assertion" and an "assessment." An assertion is a fact that can be verified; for example, it is eighty-four degrees in this room (p. 93). An assessment is "a judgment of a particular state of affairs" (p. 95).

Why are these concepts important? In organizations, people are constantly making assertions and assessments, but often do not recognize the difference. "My boss is very cold and disconnected." This is an assessment based on criteria that a person is using. Another person might in fact find the opposite because they expect different kinds of behaviour from a boss. An assertion would be, "my boss arrives at work every day at the same time."

This example illustrates the differences in social interactions. In one job, the "assessment" among staff was that top executive of the organization was remote, austere, and intellectually intimidating. The manager was advised by most staff to keep away from him and to make sure he did not meddle in his project.

Over the years, the manager had learned that the "assessments" of others were not necessarily applicable to his relationships with other executives. He built his own relationship with this executive. He turned out to be of enormous support, notwithstanding a few idiosyncrasies that were not particularly bothersome. In fact, when he ran into major trouble with another superior, the supposed austere executive was the one who solved the problem. The dynamics of working relationships can be very different, depending on personality, background, the issues at hand, and common interests.

Do not confuse *assertions and assessments*. Recognize when you are making an assessment and that you are looking at someone, or an issue, through a lens of your own values, personality, etc. An extrovert may find a manager to be closed, but she may simply be quiet and reflective. An introvert may react to a chatty manager negatively because he is always talking about subjects such as his family or vacation and it seems too casual and personal. Both are making assessments rather than assertions.

Another fascinating concept used by Flaherty is what he calls the "structure of interpretation." He argues that language is very important to how people define themselves and the world. The structure of interpretation is the way we see the world (p. 25). This is developed over our lifetime and is based on our life experiences. Flaherty argues that the "structure of interpretation determines the actions we take" and it is often "invisible" to us. A key role for an executive coach is to help the client be aware of the structure of his/her interpretation and to make observations that might help to unlock a problematic situation or behaviour pattern (p. 26).

One example would be a manager who says: "I am just a little fish," and this interpretation makes it difficult for the manager to be assertive in management meetings with superiors, even though he or she has a lot to say.

A coach would explore how the manager develops this idea, or whether it is also applicable to other parts of his/her life and help to reframe this structure of interpretation. This should enable the manager to see him/herself in a different light and then act accordingly.

Another example might be a manager who says: "I always do what I am asked to do 100 percent, no matter what it takes. I am the person who must accept total responsibility for the organization." This is a tall task, and this way of interpreting his role is probably deeply rooted in his personality and career history. But, it can also lead to some very damaging tendencies such as being a workaholic, micromanaging staff, and failing to maintain a work-family balance.

The essence of coaching—using the methods developed by Flaherty and New Ventures West—is to help managers to reflect upon and assess the structure of their interpretation against what they want to achieve. Often coaches will use new metaphors (e.g., dolphin instead of little fish), that will help managers bridge themselves to a new structure of interpretation. In difficult cases, this may require exercises to help develop new behaviours and several coaching sessions to assess progress and provide new challenges.

A good example of this "structure of interpretation" concept is a manager who was part of a tour of organizations organized by the Conference Board of Canada to assess quality. This group visited organizations in Washington, Wisconsin, Phoenix, and Utah. One manager was a police chief in Madison, Wisconsin. He had developed a top-quality police force with a strong community policing approach. Their organization had received a top-ranked national quality service award in the United States.

He described his transformation as a leader by using a single example. He said that he always believed that: "If something is to be done right, do it yourself." Unfortunately, he found that this approach resulted in constant complaints about his decisions, and his job was not much fun. Finally, he faced a very clear task of ordering new police cars. He did not want to go through yet another round of constant complaining about his decision.

He decided that his way of looking at this or the "structure of his interpretation" needed to be changed. He delegated the whole task to a group of police officers who reviewed vehicles and then decided on the appropriate model within a budget. He had no idea what would happen and was not very comfortable as the process unfolded. He even considered pulling back the authority of the working group. However, the approach worked wonders. The policemen got involved, took their responsibility seriously, and made a good decision. The complaints disappeared. He said: "That was the end of my do-it-yourself style."

After that, he engaged his organization constantly in taking responsibility for decisions; as a result, the quality of the police force increased immensely, as did their capacity to work with the community. The result was that his police force won a prestigious national quality award. Incidentally, his quality of life improved because he was not taking on every decision himself and bearing the full weight of responsibility for every operational detail of the police force.

This police chief had thus changed his original "structure of interpretation," which was probably based on an assessment that other individuals, and especially groups, were incapable of doing the job—which turned out to be incorrect.

The depth and skill of trained coaches to be able to understand the total person (e.g., view of self; relations with others; link to community; health) is startling. The author has had the opportunity to take a course with James Flaherty and attend two weeks of coaching training, following the New Ventures approach. It was a deep and sometimes unsettling experience to realize just how much difference there is among individuals and how they view themselves and the world. It was also hard to recognize that organizations are much more than processes, policies, and people doing their jobs; there is a full array of emotions at play and an amazing variety of "structures of interpretation" at work in an organization.

As young professionals join the workplace and either work with managers or become supervisors or managers, they need to be able to reflect on themselves and their structure of interpretation and to understand the depth of feelings that are present in the work environment (fear, uncertainty, joy, confidence, doubt) along with cognitive processes.

If you do not have direct access to executive coaching, there are other ways to take advantage of the advances in this area, such as courses or books and by continuous observation and self-assessment. Drawing on the insights of executive coaching will help young professionals and aspiring managers better to navigate in the world of management and to develop a manag erial identity that will enable them to lead organizations successfully. This can also help to maintain a healthy balance with other aspects of their lives.

Given the challenges that managers face today, executive coaching is now becoming a necessity for those who are struggling in their jobs. Organizations have recognized this and are putting executive coaches on staff and making them available to senior managers and to staff who are on the management track. The same can be said of mentoring. Managers find they are very alone in their jobs and need advice and wisdom from colleagues or others who have faced similar challenges. Managers at any level should seek out mentors or learn by watching others at work so as to build more perspective on their jobs and deepen their learning.

One of the last sessions of the course is devoted to executive coaching. When available, an executive coach such as Paul Lefebvre will join our class to share his or her insights into the issues coaches face in working with managers and to challenge students to reflect on how they view themselves within organizations.

Conclusion

This Guide started with three examples of managers: Diane Lavoie, chief of enforcement in Fisheries; Jacob Martin, director of policy at Aboriginal Affairs; and Ron Storie, general manager of the Heritage Golf Course.

All three of these managers are examples of the main focus of the Politics of Management course. They all face the same dilemmas and challenges that Linda Hill describes in her book *Becoming a Manager*. They face the task of defining their roles as managers and learning how to balance the overall relationships with staff, superiors, and other groups, all within the context of managing an organization.

By applying the concepts of this course and using the "Thinking Like a Manager" framework and the suggested strategies in this part of the Guide, these managers should be able to make some sense out of the complex tapestry of relationships and trends that they face, and determine a path forward. With some reflection on themselves and their relationships with key groups, peers, and superiors, they should be able to develop their managerial identity and become effective managers leading productive organizations.

SECTION V

Politics of Management Course: Design and Major Lessons

5.0 Overview

This last section brings together the major insights of the course and then outlines how it aims to help students "think like managers."

The centrepiece of the course is the framework for "thinking like a manager" and the key concepts that it identifies. This course can be boiled down into this one chart in Section II, which can be used to assess managers and the challenges they face as well as some of the key tools or concepts that they should use to develop a management strategy or agenda.

5.1 Design of the Politics of Management Course

The Politics of Management course has been designed for people who are working with managers, or expect to be in managerial positions responsible for staff and a management agenda. The Politics of Management course aims to simulate the realities of management, provide students with some key concepts and insights, and help them meet the challenge of developing and managing effective and productive organizations.

The author has taught this course for twenty-five years. Feedback from students (most of whom are part-time students already working in government and non-profit organizations) shows that, at this early stage in their careers, they are interested in learning the basic concepts, tools, and insights that they can apply immediately to their work.

For this reason, the course uses a combination of techniques such as development of concepts, cases, field research, and questions that focus on skill-building in certain areas. The aim is to learn a framework for analysis, understand useful concepts, and apply them to real situations. The course helps students advance their learning and knowledge of management in general, as well as meeting their own personal challenges as present and future executives.

The core focus of this course is: what does it take for managers to be effective in their jobs? It deals with the complex, dynamic, and often disorganized world that managers face, and how they must deal with these realities. This course will enable students to work on real practical management issues and challenges and reflect on their own experiences in management.

Authors like Mintzberg have argued that classic MBA programs do not help to develop managers. In his work reviewing the needs of managers compared to what MBA programs usually provide, he has concluded that programs aiming to develop executives should focus on areas required for managers such as skills, intuition, and diagnosis. Mintzberg argued that a major part of management development should be learning how to diagnose the complex situations that managers face, developing descriptive insight and skills that relate to the softer processes of intuition, and learning how managers make decisions. He also argued for extensive use of fieldwork and involvement in projects relating to management (Mintzberg, *Managing*, pp. 118–19).

This course—the Politics of Management—reflects many of Mintzberg's suggestions.

Linda Hill, *Becoming a Manager* (pp. 264–66), did extensive research on first-time managers over their first year in the job. She concluded that "management is an art requiring a mix of talents." She argues that:

> Since managing change has become more significant, the need has grown for managers to possess conceptual skills—the ability to make sense of and establish direction from overwhelming and often ambiguous (or conflicting) data. The human competencies required for management have continued to grow in significance with the increased need to exercise influence without formal authority and build and lead effective teams capable of adapting and innovating.

Later in the book, she notes that "to be effective managers must be prepared to learn about themselves (their identities, strengths, and limitations), be willing to make necessary changes, and cope with the associated stress and emotions" (p. 267).

Other authors, including Chris Argyris, have discussed the need for executives to become more self-aware and be able to reflect on their own selves. They need to reflect on how they manage others and to understand how they approach problems and influence decision-making. Argyris has found executives to be surprisingly unable to modify counterproductive behaviour, change their mental maps, and reflect on their style and method of solving problems. Many techniques are available these days to help managers assess their management style, including Myers-Briggs surveys and upward feedback. (Refer to Chris Argyris and Donald A. Schön, *Organizational Learning: A Theory of Action Perspective*, pp. 109–27.)

Finally, some schools, such as the Harvard Kennedy School of Government and the Harvard Business School, have adopted an approach to the development of executives that uses multiple experiences based on case analyses. This approach relies on exposing students to many different situations and letting them develop ways to approach issues and decisions. The advantage of this approach is that it encourages students to think like managers and work with the complex, confusing situations that managers often face.

The design for this course is a hybrid approach including: key concepts; overall framework; case approach; assessment; self-reflection on management style; and studies of real-life managers.
Five methods are used to achieve the course objectives:

- The use of specific analytical and diagnostic skills in analyzing the external and organizational environment, or power mapping

- The development of knowledge of key concepts involving how managers make choices within the context of multiple roles and agendas and deal with pressures and conflicts (these concepts are drawn from readings in the public and private sectors)

- The assessment of management and operating styles of managers and how this can impact their effectiveness as executives; and the assessment of management styles, or work experiences of students

- The application of these concepts and skills to the discussion and analysis of cases and management issues, or specific managerial jobs in government and non-profit organizations

- The integration of the case experiences and key course concepts with the experiences and challenges faced by individual students in organizational environments

The best way to learn to "think like a manager" is to discuss the choices that managers can make in diverse management situations and organizations. Management requires a certain agility to adapt to different organizations and situations and determine the best approach for that particular situation.

For this reason, this course covers different management challenges in government and not-for-profit organizations.

The course includes cases involving a variety of organizations where managers are faced with a number of issues and choices. In addition, there is a final assignment that is mandatory and that requires students to review the entire course, their own personal experience and insights; to determine what they learned about management; and their perspectives on management through the course.

5.2 Major Lessons of the Course

This course is aimed primarily to help government and non-profit staff make a successful transition to management roles or to learn how to work with managers in their positions as policy advisors, program analysts, etc.

Each student, depending on interests, experience, and ambition derives different lessons from this course. There are, however, five general lessons relating largely to the transition for first-time managers and managerial roles that will be highlighted below.

- **Management is managing relationships or getting work done through people and groups.**

One of our first readings in this course was Hill's *Becoming a Manager*, where she describes the difficulties managers face in developing their identity and defining their role. Hill found that managers, early in their careers, tend to focus on the task, as opposed to building the organization and relationships that make it possible for the organization to succeed. Hill also found that new managers face significant difficulties managing subordinates and in their relationships with superiors.

This course aims clearly to demonstrate that managers work in the middle of a web of relationships and issues present in the organizational and external environments; and that it is he/she who has to make decisions on how to achieve the work of the organization.

Management is the art of organizing people to accomplish the functions of an organization. To develop and achieve an agenda, it is critical to develop sources of influence through relationships and networks.

This capacity can be developed through preparation, observation, and self-development. Those who aspire to move into management positions should develop this capacity by working as part of a team, taking responsibility to lead projects, and continuously learning from role models in organizations.

- **The management job is more and more difficult: management is a tough job.**

Kotter shows the enormous complexity and challenges of modern-day management jobs, and the complex, uncertain, and difficult environment in which managers must operate. As much as possible, the cases included in this course illustrate this point.

Through the years, complexity and interdependence have increased exponentially, and managers and executives are now faced with high levels of interdependency and low levels of clear authority. In this environment, the need to develop a viable agenda is greater than ever, amid intense coordination with many parties and a complex network of relationships.

This is true in the private sector, as companies merge, split, and face rapid changes in technology. It is also true in government, with the increasing complexity and constraints and the constant challenge of working with the political system. Managers in non-profit organizations also face significant challenges in doing their jobs effectively in a changing business and government environment, and a continuously changing society.

To respond to these challenges, managers need to develop the capacity and skills to assess their total environment and the potential to achieve an agenda. New managers need quickly to develop an ability to assess the broader environment that they may not have been exposed to in earlier jobs.

These skills can be developed through analysis, but also by learning from senior executives who have this capacity. First-time managers will have a much higher probability of success if they are able to assess their environment, their dependency relationships, the agendas of government, or the agendas of top executives in non-profit organizations.

- **Managers have to understand *power and influence to be effective, as well as their limitations and assets*.**

To be a good manager, you have to know organizational dynamics and power relationships, as follows:

Going into a job, you must recognize your assets and your power gaps. Several cases in the course address serious problems with management style and available power. The reality is that getting anything done in a complex, uncertain organization full of constraints is a challenge. So it is essential to figure out how to build and lever your agenda.

Linda Hill found that first-time managers tend to be uncomfortable with the "politics" in their jobs in their transition to management positions. They also had difficulty dealing with the reality that their authority was insufficient to carry out their job even with subordinates. They had to build the credibility and influence to enable them to exercise enough power to get the job done.

A major lesson in this course is that managers must learn how to develop the required power to do their jobs and that they cannot rely on the authority that comes with a new management position.

- **Success is possible: Managers can succeed and get great satisfaction in doing their jobs. But you have to be good at it and like it—or it will frustrate you enormously.**

After several cases in the Politics of Management course and some lively discussions of the challenges faced by leaders of organizations, students are often shocked at how difficult these jobs can be. They also wonder if these jobs can be performed successfully. The unequivocal answer is: success is possible. One of the main purposes of this course is to provide the perspective, the framework, the concepts, and some of the tools that will enable new managers to be successful in a complex and challenging organizational environment.

Management requires abilities to create meaning in an organization, articulate an agenda, and work with a wide variety of players to achieve that agenda. People who like to do this enjoy leading organizations, building teams, improving organizational performance, and managing change.

Leading an organization can be similar to the thrill of developing and coaching a sports team where the coach gets all the players working together, maximizing their abilities and winning championships.

On the other hand, organizations are littered with managers who do not really want to be managers, who kind of fell into it, and who have not taken the time to learn what is effective, or to have an understanding of their styles. On the positive side, there are many great management jobs in government, as well as in the private sector. Some people will get a lot of satisfaction in carrying them out and will make a significant difference for governments, business, or non-profit organizations and their staff.

For first-time managers, their first job can be simply overwhelming—especially if they have not prepared for this new role. To succeed as a first-time or middle manager, it is important to begin preparing early in your career through taking leadership courses, doing some self-assessment regarding management style, and continual learning from other successful managers. Mentors are also exceptionally useful. Generally, a manager will develop a managerial identity in his or her first year on the job, but will face enormous struggles in defining that identity. By starting early in your career, you will have much more time to reflect and learn and be ready for a managerial role.

- **Managers have to learn how to manage their relationship with their boss and understand their own leadership style.**

Just about every case in this course deals with the managers' leadership style, how they make decisions, how they work with superiors or subordinates, and how they build teams. It is critical to understand the kinds of choices your superiors make and how they define their operational style. This will enable managers to develop an effective strategy for working with superiors.

As part of understanding how to work with superiors, you have to also develop your capacity to understand your own leadership style and your strengths and weaknesses.

In developing your capacities, learn to assess how superiors adapt their styles to various challenges and whether they are effective. This will enrich your range of understanding of what works and what does not work for various people and situations.

First-time managers seem to have a great deal of ambivalence in managing their relationships with superiors. First, there is often a lot of reluctance to be active in developing the relationship required. There is a tendency to be passive and wait for the superior to define either the agenda of the organization or how work will be carried out. In becoming a manager, it is important to learn how to forge a strong common agenda and a working relationship with superiors. This by itself is a huge asset in achieving an agenda and managing the organization successfully.

- **To achieve an agenda, a manager must maximize alignment and eliminate non-alignment.**

A key lesson that will be developed in the course is to make strategic choices concerning how far and how fast you can proceed with your agenda. Sometimes, all the lights are green, and you can really move an agenda forward quickly. Other times, a manager has to build sufficient power to move forward effectively.

When all the forces are going in a specific and clear direction, or an opportunity emerges, managers should maximize alignment with those forces and "ride the wave" for change, just as a surfer would do with a huge ocean wave.

Most management jobs involve demands and pressures that far exceed the capacity of the manager or staff to handle. It is vital to be sure of your priorities and know which are immediately critical, and in which sequence. Pick your spots carefully. Sometimes this means strengthening your power and influence through a series of small steps and building sufficient momentum to achieve your full agenda. You have to align your priorities with others and build partnerships with them; but also, when you have to fight, you need to pick your battles very carefully.

It is often difficult for new managers to understand just how many groups, individuals, events, or situations can derail an agenda. It is very easy for first-time managers to overestimate their probability of success because they are not sufficiently aware of the dependency relationships involved, or how essential it is to create the necessary alignment to achieve the agenda.

A first-time manager cannot afford to establish an ambitious agenda that crashes due to some obvious dependency on another group. It is important that a new manager succeed and build a reputation as an effective manager as soon as possible. For this reason, it is critical to conduct a realistic assessment of the alignments necessary to accomplish an agenda.

- **Managers must develop and understand their own leadership style and develop their managerial identity.**

As Linda Hill has noted, first-time managers have difficulty developing a managerial identity; that identity usually comes through direct experience in managing.

A key insight from her research on first-time managers is that most, if not all, of these managers go through a very difficult transition and experience considerable anxiety about their roles and competence. They struggle with their identity as a leader of a group, as opposed to an individual contributor. They also struggle with their role in evaluating staff and setting the overall direction for their organization.

One major lesson from Hill's research is that the challenges faced by first-time managers are relatively predictable. Managers generally work through these difficulties and establish an effective role for themselves.

To develop this managerial identity, it is important that managers do some assessment of their personality and tendencies in developing a team and making decisions. If possible, this should be done early in their careers and well before accepting managerial roles. The four major choices regarding the operating style of managers outlined in Section III will help in that regard.

The best approach to management development is a mixture of experience, reflection, and continuous learning both from literature and studies and from other managers. Through this approach, a first-time manager can quickly build a managerial identity and establish a level of performance that only long-time, experienced managers can achieve.

Thus, this course will strongly encourage students to assess themselves and their relationships and constantly review their performance and get feedback.

This course includes a session on the operating style of managers based on Section III of this book, as well as a class on executive coaching. These classes will help students to understand the challenges managers face today and the ways in which coaches are assisting in their development.

Since management is largely learned from experience, young professionals and aspiring managers should also seek out mentors and draw from their wisdom and experience.

5.3 Conclusions:
Why this Course Is Important for Students in Public Policy and Administration

Thinking like a manager (or executive, or leader) requires thinking about

- Your role as a manager

- Your relationships with superiors, subordinates, and colleagues

- The overall environment

- How much authority you have

- How you can exercise influence over key people and groups

It also means thinking about yourself, your management style, your credibility, and your approach to decision-making. Finally, it means

1. Developing an agenda

2. Building a network of key people and groups

3. Implementing that agenda through the network

The art of leading and directing productive organizations today requires tremendous skills in understanding organizations and their environment. Managers must develop a coalition, or alignment, of the key groups to get the organization's work done or to achieve a particular agenda. Successful managers must learn to overcome the power gaps and conflicts that are characteristic of modern organizations. They must rely on their leadership skills to develop synergy and alignment among all of the key factors and influence others to achieve a particular change or agenda.

Throughout this Guidebook, we have referred to three examples of first-time managers: Jacob Martin, a newly appointed policy director with sixteen staff; Diane Lavoie, chief of a fisheries enforcement group of twelve; and Ron Storie, general manager of a non-profit organization.

Based on the research of Linda Hill and the experiences of many executive coaches, it is likely that all three of these first-time managers will face serious issues determining their roles, working with their teams and superiors, and developing their managerial identities.

This course aims to help first-time managers like Diane, Ron, and Jacob to assess their managerial situation and develop an effective approach to managing their organizations and developing their managerial identities.

At the beginning of this Guide, students of the Politics of Management course indicated how useful this course was for them when working with managers in government and non-profit organizations. Typical comments from former students over the years:

When I got a management job, I found that I really used some of the key concepts and the framework used in the course to analyze my challenges. The Politics of Management really helped me get my agenda straight and figure out how to manage my group.

The Politics of Management course was by far the most useful course I took in the MPPA program. It is the one I used in my management role with the City of Ottawa. I am still using the basic lessons of this course ten years later.

In over twenty-five years of teaching this course, many students have approached me years later with exactly those words. This feedback from former students tells me that this course is succeeding in meeting its primary objectives. And that is why I keep teaching and developing this course year after year.

APPENDIX A

Key Course Concepts

This appendix outlines and defines some of the key concepts used in The Politics of Management course. These concepts are tools for analyzing the case studies and developing managerial strategies. They are also useful for studies of managers.

Politics

Politics "involves activities which attempt to influence decisions over critical issues that are not readily resolved through the introduction of new data and in which there are differing views. Political activity is activity which is undertaken to overcome some resistance or opposition. Thus, politics is really the process of building and gaining support from various individuals or groups and inevitably includes influencing others." (Jeffrey Pfeffer, *Power in Organizations*, p.7)

The politics of management is therefore defined as the activities that executives carry out in order to influence others to achieve their agenda and the aims of the organization.

Power

"It is generally agreed that power characterizes relationships among social actors. Most definitions of power include an element indicating that power is the capability of one social actor to overcome resistance in achieving a desired object or result . . . power is a relation among social actors in which one social actor 'A' can get another social actor 'B' to do something that 'B' would not otherwise have done." (pp. 2–3)

In this course, power is viewed as a neutral concept. Power can be used wisely and can be absolutely necessary to achieve the aims of the organization or society. In the wrong hands, too much power can also lead to negative results. In this course, we assume that the aim of maximizing power for the leaders of organizations is to achieve a productive organization or the positive agenda of the leaders. Power is in many ways the sum of authority and influence.

Power Gap

A power gap is a major gap between the amount of power needed to achieve an agenda or a particular job and the amount of power that the executive actually has. As Kotter indicates, authority is limited for most managers and is not sufficient to achieve an agenda in most complex organizations. When pursuing an agenda, many of the groups on which the manager depends are outside the manager's chain of command. Even with the staff reporting to a manager there can be limits to the effectiveness of authority. Understanding power gaps is therefore a critical skill in developing and implementing an agenda.

Authority

"The distribution of power within a social setting can also be legitimated over time, so that those within that setting expect and value a certain pattern of influence. When power is so legitimated, it is denoted as authority . . . The transformation of power into authority is an important process, for it speaks to the issue of the institutionalization of social control." (p. 4)

In organizations, authority is often established through positions or roles or history and culture. However, as Kotter has pointed out, direct authority in most complex organizations is limited and not sufficient to achieve the agendas of the organization or leader.

Dependency and Dependency Relationship

"The argument that the organization is a coalition of support implies that an important factor determining the organization's behaviour is the dependencies on the various coalition participants. Three factors are critical in determining the dependence of one organization on another. First, there is the importance of the resource, the extent to which the organization requires it for continued operation and survival. The second is the extent to which the interest group has discretion over the resource allocation and use. And, third, the extent to which there are few alternatives, or the extent of control over the resource by the interest group, is an important factor determining the dependence of the organization." (Pfeffer, *The External Control of Organizations: A Resource Dependence Perspective*, pp. 45–46)

As Kotter has indicated, given the interdependence of organizations and the importance of players to the executive's agenda, it is critical to understand the degree of dependence on others. Most complex organizations are faced with multiple dependency relationships that must be defined and understood clearly, and executives must develop strategies for gaining co-operation and support where required.

Accountability

Accountability is the obligation to answer to a person or group for the exercise of responsibilities conferred. Accountability involves the fundamental question of who is responsible for what and to whom. According to this definition, people are accountable only to those individuals or groups with whom they have a direct authority relationship based on legislation, convention, or organizational hierarchy. It is important to note that the concept of accountability is much more precise than more general concepts such as responsibility to someone or being answerable to someone. (G. Osbaldeston, *Keeping Deputy Ministers Accountable*, p. 5)

Obviously, knowing to whom the manager is accountable will help him/her design an agenda and identify demands, choices, and requirements for managing the relationship with that person (i.e., the boss).

Demands

Demands are what anyone in the job has to do. There are many things that a manager ought to do because they are in the job description, or because his or her boss thinks them important, but demands "are only what must be done." (Stewart, *Choices for the Manager*, p. 2)

For this course, I like to think of demands as the three or four tasks that a manager absolutely must do if he/she is to be viewed as doing his/her job. These are the basic expectations of bosses, the firm, or others that must be fulfilled if the person is to carry out his/her basic responsibilities. For example, think of performance appraisal time when the manager is meeting with his/her superior. What are the three or four tasks (maximum) that the manager should have done to keep the job and be viewed as a high performer?

Constraints

Constraints are "the factors internal or external to the organization that limit what the jobholder can do." (Stewart, *Choices for the Manager*, p. 2) Constraints can consist of resource limitations or legal, technological, cultural, organizational, and political limitations. Constraints are not just objective impediments. They are a combination of real obstacles and subjective perceptions of obstacles.

While many managers can find constraints everywhere they look, others can work around every constraint that comes up without even slowing down. Why? One of the major challenges for managers is to decide which constraints they should accept, which ones they should challenge, and which ones they should simply avoid. This often requires a good understanding of the systems that the manager is working with; moreover, the manager must understand his/her own tendencies to follow rules, ignore rules, or manage rules.

Choices

According to Rosemary Stewart in *Choices for the Manager* (pp. 17–24), choices involve the decisions managers can make about doing their jobs where they have some discretion. This can involve choices about the degree of delegation, the focus of the group in relation to other groups, and the degree of focus on technical as opposed to the overall management of the group. One of the major points in Stewart's work is that managers are not sufficiently aware of the choices they have and do not often take advantage of some of the opportunities that exist for choices.

Stewart points out that in managerial jobs, there are major choices in what aspects of the job are emphasized, what tasks to focus on, the degree of work-sharing or delegation, and the extent to which the jobholder concentrates on the traditional domain for the job or focuses on adding new areas of responsibility.

Choice: Work-sharing

Work-sharing, as described by Rosemary Stewart in *Choices for the Manager* (pp. 50–53), involves the sharing of work responsibilities or tasks between a manager and his/her superiors, subordinates, and colleagues. It is one of the areas of choices that managers can make with respect to how they carry out their jobs. Work-sharing can be an important strategy for building alliances, sharing responsibility, or enabling a manager to pursue particular priorities.

Choice: Boundary management

Boundary management involves the management of the relationship between the unit for which the manager is responsible and the groups or activities outside the unit. Managers often make important choices with respect to how they manage these relationships. For example, some may be active in managing the interface between the organization and outside groups, and others may be passive.

> Managers who are aware of this choice will seek to maintain or to improve the conditions within which the unit operates. Their efforts may need to be focused upon their boss, other senior managers, staff and service departments, suppliers and customers, whether inside or outside the organization . . ." (Stewart, *Choices for the Manager*, p. 25)

Dominant Coalition

The dominant coalition is "the personal characteristics and the internal relationships of that minimum group of co-operating employees who oversee the organization as a whole and control its basic policy-making." (Kotter, *Organizational Dynamics*, p. 20)

One can discover the dominant coalition not by organizational charts but by determining the groups of people who have to be involved and agree before major decisions are made. If one were to take ten major decisions and find out who was involved, there would usually be a few dominant players who would be critical to all the decisions. Dominant coalitions can vary tremendously in organizations. Obviously, understanding the dominant coalition is important for managers in analyzing how they can achieve an agenda.

Alignment and Non-Alignment

When an organization's key systems have characteristics that fit together, are congruent, consistent and co-aligned, one usually finds there are efficient processes at work and a relatively stable equilibrium. This usually means there is alignment in the organization. When there are significant imbalances or contradictions between, for example, the demands of the external environment and the organizational structure, there is a non-alignment. This usually leads to disequilibrium and changes. (Kotter, *Organizational Dynamics*, p.39)

Heroic Manager

This term, used by David L. Bradford and Allan R. Cohen in *Managing for Excellence*, (pp. 10–17), means the following:

A heroic manager is a person who sees himself or herself as being the person responsible for the future direction and tasks of the organization. Heroic managers figure they must understand what is going on in the department at all times. They should have more technical expertise than any subordinate. They must be able to solve any problem that comes along, and they should be the primary, if not the only, person responsible for how the department is operating.

The tendency of the heroic manager to crave complete responsibility and control may create major dysfunctions in an organization. This management style can limit the free flow of information, undermine the staff's sense of responsibility and create an organization that is limited by the creativity and energy of one person, as well as major bottlenecks that reduce the organization's ability to adjust to change.

Heroic managers usually create an environment that results in lower-quality decisions and motivation problems with employees. The best employees usually leave because they cannot grow and develop without being able to assume responsibility, take risks, and make mistakes — which the heroic manager won't allow.

The heroic manager's style often creates a self-fulfilling cycle where the manager accepts more and more responsibility and subordinates back away from responsibility . . . often reducing their performance. The result is that the heroic manager works harder and harder to make up for the gaps and eventually falls victim to his/her limitations. (See p. 17)

Post-Heroic Manager

Manager as developer: Bradford and Cohen, *Managing for Excellence* (pp. 60–62)

The post-heroic leader believes that an organization's success is the result of teamwork and co-operation of staff and shared responsibility. At the same time, as the "manager works to develop management responsibility in subordinates, he/she must develop the subordinates' abilities to share the management of the unit's performance." (Bradford and Cohen, *Managing for Excellence*, pp. 60–61) The manager takes the view that "only when subordinates become skilled in the managerial tasks required for total departmental success can the sharing of responsibility lead to excellence." (p. 61)

Rather than depending on heroic rides-to-the-rescue — with all the answers and total responsibility — they have sought the far greater power and potential for excellence available in the commitment and abilities of their whole group. (p. 61) These managers have in mind a developmental, collaborative, galvanizing, but subordinate-centred image. (p. 61)

Espoused Theories and Theories—in-action (Argyris)

Argyris distinguishes between "espoused theory" and "theory-in-use." The former is the theory of action to which a manager gives allegiance, and which, upon request, he communicates to others. However, the theory that actually governs his actions is his "theory-in-use," which may or may not be compatible with his "espoused" theory. Furthermore, the individual may or may not be aware of the incompatibility of the two theories. (*Organizational Learning: A Theory of Action Perspective*, p.11)

Force Field Analysis

This term refers to the assessment of the potential for change. (Beckhard and Harris, *Organizational Transitions*) Before deciding on an intervention strategy, the manager needs to determine the amount of control or influence he/she has over the causes or conditions providing the stimulus for changing in the first place. To do this, he or she could do a force field analysis.

> "On one axis we can list the sources of the forces pressing on the management that are pushing toward a change . . . and on the other axis we can identify the potency of the force. Management can then array the nature of the forces operating in the situation." . . . Using the length of arrows, one can then indicate the strength of these forces for and against a particular direction. (p. 29)

Differentiation and Integration

These two concepts are very important for understanding the challenges of managing organizations and their dynamics.

Jay Galbraith, in *Designing Complex Organizations*, describes differentiation as the organization of various sub-tasks in the organization. This is usually equated with some common elements of the tasks involved and a division of labour. (p. 3) For example, a department of health might have highly differentiated groups consisting of scientists doing research, program groups promoting health outcomes, and administrative and information technology staff. All of these groups would involve different occupational groups and operational functions.

The other dimension involves the various approaches used to bring together the organization to achieve the overall objectives. The fundamental dynamic that he describes is that the more differentiation, the greater the challenge in finding ways to achieve integration. Throughout the book, he describes various ways to achieve this end, such as common objectives; information and planning systems; lateral relations; and ad hoc co-operation across specialty groups.

These concepts are useful for managing organizations because if a manager is faced with a highly differentiated organization with little cohesion and little interest in co-operating to achieve a common purpose, the management challenge will be considerable.

APPENDIX B

Guidelines for
Case Preparation

Overview

The objective of using cases in this course is to give students an opportunity to wrestle with examples of situations faced by managers. By working with these realistic case situations, students get a sense of the role of managers and the choices they face.

The cases also provide an opportunity to apply the concepts and framework for the course to develop the strategies required to manage the organization. The guidelines are aimed at providing students with some ideas on how to approach case analysis and the development of a case memo and attachment.

Reading, Analyzing, and Discussing a Case

Management cases are by their nature complex puzzles that involve a lot of players, issues, and events. They require students to deal with the realities of governments or non-profits as managers find them and to determine an approach that is workable.

It is best to read the case a couple of times and then leave it for a few days and think about it. You are encouraged to discuss the case with fellow students to develop your thinking. The actual memo and attachments should be done by individual students.

The cases for the Politics of Management course are quite different than cases you might find in other courses. Many cases for public administration or business administration are focused on functional areas such as marketing, financial management, operations management, or policy issues. For this reason, they may have only a few dimensions and seldom focus on the total environment faced by managers or executives.

The cases for this course are focused on the real world of executives who are working within organizations, dealing with complex and often controversial issues. They deal simultaneously with the challenges of working with superiors, subordinates, clients, and fellow colleagues, as well as short- and long-term issues. In the world of management, there are few decisions or actions that do not require the consideration of all of these variables at the same time.

When reviewing or discussing the case, it is suggested that you start with the manager involved, his or her background, skills, or management style, and the particular challenges or power gaps. The case should be reviewed through the eyes of the executive who is trying to establish or accomplish an agenda in the context of an organization and various relationships. The objective of the memo should be to help the executive meet the requirements of the job and build credibility, reputation, and the capacity to achieve the requirements of the organization.

Apply the Course Concepts to the Case

The concepts developed in this course have been distilled over the years to be the most useful and practical tools available to assess complex management situations. If you spend the time to learn and use these concepts, you will find that they will not only help in the case analysis but they will be useful for years to come in many different organizational situations.

Many students of this course who are now consultants, senior executives, or managers have told me that of all the courses they have taken at Carleton University, the framework for this course and its key concepts have been the most useful in tackling the realities of their jobs. Some have even successfully obtained their first job using these concepts.

In reviewing the case, you should take some of the main concepts, such as demands, constraints and choices, power gap, dependency relationship, and alignment and use them to understand the case and develop the strategy.

The key to most of the cases is to understand the constraints, the demands, the opportunities for action or alignment of people or initiatives. The best way to remember concepts is to use them. Cases or a study of a manager are the most practical ways of using them. Another way is to discuss issues that you are facing in the work environment and to apply the concepts. This will also be encouraged in class.

It is suggested that you start with the attachment and write up your analysis of the case and use of concepts before starting the memo. This approach often leads you to insights that you will not achieve by trying to write the memo first and then the attachment.

The Case Analysis and Memo

The cases will include a case question that is aimed at encouraging students to think about the case. However, the specific case assignment is included in the course outline. The reason for this is that the cases remain relatively constant over time, but the professor changes the case questions depending on the design of the course. Always follow the case assignment in the course outline.

Based on the feedback from the most recent Politics of Management courses, I have redesigned the case analysis requirements for the course. The main reason for this is that few students have case study experience and many face initial challenges in writing memos that deal with the complexity of the management environment and the strategies required to respond to this environment.

The first two cases in the course are development cases focused on building the skills of students to analyze a complex management situation using the "thinking like a manager" framework and to develop skills in power mapping. The questions included in each of these cases are fairly straightforward. After discussing the responses of students, the professor will outline the strategies required for a manager in these situations and the type of memo that would be required.

Case Memo

After the first two cases, for all the other cases, a memo or Power Point presentation focused on advice for the manager involved in the case.

Students often ask: What does a memo look like? Do you have guidelines on how to write the memo? The short answer is no. However, there are a few tips you should keep in mind.

- The memo is usually written from someone to the executive, or by the executive to their superior. A simple, To: Deputy Minister . . . From: John Smith, Director General of Fisheries, Operations is sufficient. This format, often used in government memos, is all that is required. It should be signed as if you were the DG or ADM involved.

- In writing the memo, keep in mind the personality and management style and agenda of the person to whom you are writing.

- Don't spend a lot of time (more than half a page) describing the situation in the case. Only mention the highlights and assume the reader knows the case situation.

- Your memo should be specific enough so that the reader knows what action needs to be taken and the probability that it will work. There should be a comfort level that the challenges have been thought through and can be implemented. If the executive you are briefing has raised particular issues or concerns, make sure you address them. An example of something that doesn't work would be an initiative that requires someone's support (dependency relationship) and you have not addressed how you would get that support. Another example would be a plan for action that does not fit the agenda or management style of your superior.

- One mistake that students often make is that they cover part of the challenges facing the manager and forget about other key relationships that need to be aligned for the approach to work (i.e., relationships with subordinates or other key players). Remember, for most management initiatives to work, you need to align all the players and factors that are critical to the success of the initiative or at least neutralize any opposition you may anticipate for the initiative.

- The preferred length of the memo is usually three to five single-spaced pages plus a two-page attachment. More is not better in case memos, as is the case in work situations. In government and non-profits, one of the cherished skills is the ability to write a memo or document that is concise and yet provides the information and analysis sufficient for the decision. Thus, a six-page memo that has three pages of summary of the case will not be very appealing.

Strategies

In dealing with these cases, at some point you have to decide on what your basic strategy is. Successful management strategies take into account the total situation that the manager is facing from his/her own strengths and weaknesses: the external environment; the organization and its environment; relations with superiors, subordinates, and others; the power gaps involved; and choices.

Here are some tips on strategies that students should consider when developing their approach to the case.

1. *Focus on the key demand or requirement of the job and choices.* It is easy to get distracted in a management situation by the number of issues or challenges you face. That is why it is critical to understand what the key expectation is of doing the job and the major choices you have as an executive. The demand for you to accomplish the job successfully is not always clear; or even what it is stated to be by others.

2. *Include all the players and align the agenda or strategy.* A successful strategy seldom deals with only one dimension of the manager's environment. For example, a strategy that deals well with a boss or other groups, but which does not consider alignment with subordinates, is often less effective than one that builds alignment among all the key players and dependency relationships. Similarly, a strategy that responds to some internal issues in your organization with subordinates, but does not reflect your boss's agenda, is doomed to failure.

3. *Always work from your strengths in building sufficient power to overcome power gaps and be careful not to leap into the abyss when you are vulnerable.* A common mistake in developing a strategy is to come up with a bold or interesting approach that involves a "bridge too far" when you are faced with major power gaps. On occasion, if there is a huge shift in your external environment and you need to make a huge change to meet the requirements of the situation, a bold strategy is required. In other instances, you need to carefully develop your credibility, influence, and power based on smaller steps. Likewise, you may want to use some of the techniques Kotter outlines, such as developing an agenda and building a network to support it.

The concepts or assumptions

Each case memo should be combined with an attachment of a maximum of two pages.

The attachment focuses on some concepts or readings that students have found important to the case analysis.

The attachment requires that students think through the concepts and apply them to the case. They are also an opportunity to explain any assumptions you may have about the particular manager or situation involved. Cases cannot explain everything or they would be fifty pages long. So, if there is some confusion, or there is a question that is not covered in the case, the attachment provides a way to explain a particular assumption that the student has made that affects the overall strategy.

In order to emphasize how important it is to do the case analysis and use the concepts the case mark will be 50 percent for the memo and 50 percent for the attachment.

Other than explaining some of your assumptions, the best way to do the attachment is to choose several key concepts and explain how you used them and applied them to the case. A general narrative on the overall case, without much reference to the concepts, will usually earn a B mark or less. An exceptional mark is merited by the description and application of at least half a dozen concepts with insights into how they helped to analyze the case. This can also be in point form or chart form. For example,

"I really found the concept of demand combined with power gap and agenda very useful. When I assessed the absolute requirements of doing this job, I discerned what it involved, but when combined with the power gap concept, it was clear that the manager could not meet the basic demands of the job or achieve an agenda without a strategy to increase his power and ability to influence the agenda. For that reason, I focused my strategy on achieving an agenda that met the critical demand but was feasible in terms of the amount of power that could be developed in this situation."

Class Discussion of Cases

The professor usually asks two or three people in the class to describe their approach to the case and make recommendations to start the case discussions.

The Politics of Management course is usually attended by a mixture of part-time and full-time students, most of whom have some work experience, either as co-op students or through working in the federal or provincial governments, or non-profits. On average, a typical class involves student experience in at least twelve different departments or organizations. This course aims to build on this work experience for case discussions.

For this reason, a good case discussion usually requires the full participation of lots of students in the class. This brings different perspectives and experience to the discussion. Thus, all students are expected to participate regardless of whether they completed a case analysis for that particular class.

The professor will encourage debates and role-playing among students to demonstrate the various agendas or interests of the players.

The role-playing has been one of the most interesting parts of the case discussion for students because it makes it more real. For example, you are assigned the role of a regional director meeting with the deputy minister and have to explain your strategy. Despite some initial hesitancy, most students respond exceptionally well to role-playing, and this brings to life the challenges facing the manager in the case.

Toward the end of the case discussion, the professor usually explains the approach or approaches that would work best in this situation.

The applicability and usefulness of the concepts and analysis are covered after the case discussion.

How to Study a Manager —Research Guidelines

The study of a manager can really help students to apply the concepts of the Politics of Management course to the challenges faced by a practising manager. A study of a manager can be done as part of the case course, but it usually takes too much time for most students. In order to focus on the studies of managers, the author has taught a research seminar that involved studies of managers using the framework of the Politics of Management course. This course may be offered again at some point in the future.

About 100 students have done studies of managers using these guidelines, which provide students with a better idea of the rationale for conducting these research papers, the range and types of papers that qualify, and the approach that is often the most useful for doing these studies.

To facilitate these studies, the professor will provide students with a letter introducing managers to the course, explaining the nature of the study, and promising full confidentiality, as well as the right to review the final product.

Why Study Managers?

The focus of this course is how managers work within organizations and how they can overcome the many challenges they face in getting the job done. By learning key concepts and approaches to management and applying them to cases, students are able to gain a better appreciation for what managers have to do to be effective.

By undertaking a study of a manager, students have the opportunity to apply the lessons of the course to a manager in their work environment. In a typical course with twelve to twenty students, the class can also learn from about a dozen examples of managers.

The key requirement for this study is that it must involve a manager who is supervising or directing others in an organization. Papers that involve general management issues, such as comparisons of the private and public sectors, or a study of an organization, do not meet the requirements of the course.

What Should the Study Involve?

Over the four or five times I have taught the research seminar course, students have done a tremendous variety of papers. This includes sales managers of car dealerships, general managers of information technology companies, human resource directors in departments of government, and project managers in National Defence. These studies have also included park managers, country program managers in an international development agency, entrepreneurs of small consulting firms, heads of associations, CEOs of hospitals, and school principals.

The variety of management jobs is simply amazing. The framework and concepts of the course were easily applied in these studies, resulting in excellent insights into the challenges faced by these managers.

Generally, both students and managers have enjoyed the papers and learned a lot from doing them. No paper has ever resulted in difficulties or embarrassment for a manager.

Many managers have commented very positively on the studies and often used the material afterwards. Managers, even if initially reluctant, often end up volunteering to spend more time in interviews than they had anticipated and have found it refreshing to think and talk about their jobs.

Students have found that these research studies of managers served to reinforce the key concepts and lessons. Studies done by students on themselves, or close colleagues, have been as successful as other studies.

The only studies that students have found difficult were those of their direct bosses, or of managers who were too busy to be available for interviews. Although studies of direct bosses are acceptable, one has to recognize that there are some limitations in doing such studies. Also, a very busy manager can create havoc with your schedule to produce this paper.

Do These Studies Involve an Assessment of Managers and Their Effectiveness?

A frequent question that is asked about these studies is: are students supposed to do an evaluation of the manager and his or her strengths and weaknesses or effectiveness? The simple answer is "no." The paper is meant to be analytical, not judgmental, in nature.

The aim of the paper is to apply the framework for the course outlined in "Thinking like a Manager" or other key concepts and ideas to a management job. The purpose is to understand the challenges faced by the manager and the strategies he or she uses to carry out that particular job. The furthest one should go in making judgments is to note that a particular requirement of this job seems to be X and there seems to be a gap between this requirement and what the manager sees as the key demands of the job.

Does the Research Identify the Manager or Organization by Name?

The simple answer to this is NO—absolutely not. In this world of high transparency, there are always going to be risks and sensitivities if a paper identifies the individuals involved. This may also reduce the willingness of managers to participate. Including the real name of the manager or the organization is not important to achieving the purpose of the course. If it were a principal of a high school that was being studied, the aim would be to understand the challenges faced by a principal. It just does not matter what school it was, or his or her name.

In the hundreds of papers that have been done for this course, I have never had a problem with a study of a manager—because we maintain their anonymity. Therefore, you must create a fictional name for the organization or department and for the manager.

Requirements for the Paper

The requirement of the paper is to apply the framework and concepts of the course to a manager's job. The quality of the paper will be judged on how well the student has described and analyzed the job using the literature and concepts of the course and how well the student has understood the particular challenges of the job and types of management strategies required to do the job effectively.

How students present this material is very flexible. It is the *result* that the professor is aiming to achieve, not a particular form of communication or writing.

The paper can be developed in many ways. It can be a fifteen-page, single-spaced paper with a few references. (Kotter, *Power and Influence*, p. 122) You can present the paper as a deck of slides (e.g., on PowerPoint). You can do the study as a video. Once, three students videotaped a presentation of their study of a manager; that was very effective.

You can also write the study as a case. Two students did that as part of the course, and it worked very well. The case should be written following the format recommended by this course; a teaching note should be attached analyzing the manager's situation and what he/she did do or should do.

Whatever format you choose, be sure to link your study to the "thinking like a manager" framework and key concepts. In this way, the professor will be able to determine whether you are using the course concepts. Some students make the mistake of simply describing a manager's job but not using the concepts to analyze their findings. This is insufficient.

Use of the Papers

These papers not only provide students with an opportunity to learn, they are useful for providing the professor with examples of management situations that can be used for the ongoing enrichment of the course and the cases.

I regard this course as a "live" course where knowledge is continuously developed by the professor and students. By incorporating lessons learned from these papers, the course will over time become stronger and more useful. For example, some of the cases currently used in the course have been developed in co-operation with former students.

Over the next few years, the professor wants to develop several more cases further focusing on first-time managers and supervisors. If students do not want any of their material used, they should indicate this on their paper, or raise it personally with the professor. In these cases, copies of the papers will not be kept.

Choosing a Manager

It is preferred that students contact their own manager to arrange for the study. When asking the manager for permission to do the study, it is very important to agree on some of the ground rules. At this point, provide the manager with the letter from the professor.

- The manager should agree to be available for two to three interviews and to provide some information or materials on his or her job and the organization.

- The manager may also agree to let the student interview others in the organization such as colleagues, clients, or subordinates.

- Some managers will even give students access to their schedules so that they can analyze the nature of their jobs.

- It is very useful to use a tape recorder in interviews. Out of hundreds of interviews I have conducted with deputy ministers and ministers, few have refused to be taped. Tapes allow you to review the information later and also produce very good quotes that can make a paper come alive. If the manager is uncomfortable in any way with the tape recorder, forget it.

- You can also ask the manager if he/she would feel comfortable identifying a few others who could add some additional perspectives on the challenges of the job.

- The student should agree to share the completed paper with the manager and to disguise the information to whatever degree the manager wants.

- If the manager has any difficulty with the confidentiality of the paper or the approach, students should ask the manager to contact the professor for further information or assurances.

- If the study is being done as part of a research seminar, the student might wish to ask the manager if he or she would be willing to come to class and discuss his/her management job. Usually, in a one-semester course, at least five managers will come to class.

How Should Students Go About the Study?

There is a series of very logical steps in conducting this kind of research.

Step 1: Choose the manager to be studied and do some background research.

Once you have agreed with the manager to do the study, you should gather up some general information on the organization and the job and start analyzing some of the characteristics of the job and the kinds of challenges the manager faces.

Using the "thinking like a manager" framework in Section 2 of this Guidebook and the kinds of questions outlined in that section, you should prepare some key questions that you would like to address to him or her.

Before the interview, you could send an email to the manager explaining the aim of the study and sharing with him or her the "Thinking Like a Manager" chart. This will help he or she understand the focus of study. In many instances, the manager will start thinking about his or her job using this framework and prepare for the first interview.

Step 2: Conduct the initial interview with the manager.

The first interview enables you to get some insights into the job of the manager and how he or she defines their role. In this interview, you should stick to general questions and let the manager tell you about his/her job.

You should ask questions like: What were the key challenges you faced in this job? What was your major agenda? How did your priorities fit with those of your bosses and subordinates? How did this job compare to other jobs?

All of these kinds of questions are open-ended and enable the manager to describe the job in his or her terms without being overly constrained by specific questions.

It is also useful to get some background information in the initial interview, such as: job description; organization chart; strategic or operational plan; description of the organization; and the biography of the specific manager. The assistant to the manager is usually very helpful for this purpose.

Step 3: Conduct other interviews or review key information made available.

It would be very useful if the manager were to refer you to two to three other people that could provide their perspectives on the job, particularly if you have a theme for the study such as a reorganization, a key issue, a major change, etc. This theme can then be explored in these interviews. Discussions with others will also provide an opportunity further to explore various dimensions of the "thinking like a manager" framework; or gaining some perspective on the operating style of the manager.

Step 4: Further analyze the information and the job.

This is a key step. With some information on the job and the organization, and possibly some additional interviews, the student should do a thorough analysis of the manager's job and how the manager approaches it.

It is often helpful at this point to start writing the outline of the paper because it helps to determine gaps you might have and suggest additional questions.

It is key at this point, if you have not already done so, to choose an approach to the paper, a theme or a key research question, For example, in a case of major downsizing in a private sector organization, the question might be: How did a director balance the demand from HQ and bosses to cut staff with the need to keep the organization functioning and maintaining morale?

Study Example
One study involved a principal of a new school who had to recruit an entirely new staff for opening in September. This study was fascinating. The principal came to class and explained that when he staffed the new school, he chose the teachers not for their teaching abilities but for their ability to contribute to extracurricular activities — sports, drama, etc. The reason he did not focus on teaching was that it is very hard to assess this quality for high school teachers, and generally, teachers would all be sufficiently competent. He was looking for teaching plus other potential contributions. He believed strongly that a new high school needed lots of activities to create an identity and a vibrant atmosphere and spirit. He knew what his agenda was and he succeeded. This manager came to class and the class was a major success because it illustrated how a principal, as manager, could develop and implement an agenda.

Once you have made significant progress on the theme of the paper, you are ready for the next phase. If you have not done some thinking about what the paper will look like before the final interview, you will inevitably find that when you are writing the paper, you will be saying: "Why did I not ask that question at my interview?"

The development of a chart can be a powerful way to engage a manager in reviewing his working environment and its challenges.

Students will find it very helpful to develop charts and discuss them with the manager during the final interview further to understand the manager's role and his/her job.

Step 5: Complete Your Final Interview(s).

It is hard to do a good study in less than two interviews with the manager, and there is seldom time to do more than three.

The second interview with the manager should focus on key themes that the student wants to explore (e.g., taking charge; problems in changing the organization; developing an agenda; implementing a particularly difficult aspect of an agenda; alignment problems; relations with superiors; adapting to a changing environment). Be careful to ask questions in a general and non-technical way. For example: "What kind of power gap did you face?" is not a good question. It is better to determine a way to ask the question that gets to the issue but without overusing the technical concepts of the course. In this interview, the student should probe a bit. To help interview the manager, it is very useful to develop some charts (similar to the charts in Osbaldeston's *Keeping Deputy Ministers Accountable*) that depict the manager's job and issues. This often helps focus the interview and provides the basis for the paper. By using the tape recorder you will be able to develop key quotes on various aspects of the job (e.g., relations with bosses, the environment, management choices, style). There is nothing better than using the manager's own words to describe his or her situation.

Step 6: Prepare and Finalize the Paper.

As noted earlier, there are many ways to present the paper, but the core requirements of a successful paper involve: a description of the job; an assessment of the challenges of the job using the "thinking like a manager" framework; some examples of management strategies used by the manager to get the job done or deal with a particular challenge; some insights into management style using Section 3 of this Guidebook; and, finally, some conclusions.

At some point, the paper, deck, case, or video must be prepared. When writing or developing the paper, it is really helpful to use charts illustrating the role of the manager and to use quotations where appropriate. Mask the name of the organization and manager as much as possible.

Class Discussion

The approach that has been the most successful for conducting class discussions of these studies is as follows:

In a twelve-session course, the first few classes are devoted to understanding the framework and concepts of the course. Since it takes time for students to undertake studies, classes four, five, and six might involve some specific examples of studies or guests to discuss their jobs. By the middle of the course, some students will have completed some work with managers, and they might be available to attend class.

If the student has made progress on a study, but the manager is not available to discuss the study, class presentations of the research will be organized. In these instances, the class usually involves two one-hour sessions in which the student discusses the study and the results. Usually, the student provides a brief handout to guide the class discussion. Students are invited to ask questions and provide comments. The main role of the professor is to provide any additional insights using the framework or concepts of the course. When a manager comes to class, the format is as follows:

- The student presents an overview of the study of the manager using the concepts and framework for the course. This usually takes about half an hour.

- The manager then discusses his or her job.

- Students ask questions and carry out a dialogue with the manager.

Selected Bibliography

Analyzing Organizations and Environment

Galbraith, Jay. *Designing Complex Organizations.* Addison–Wesley Publishing Company, 1973.

Kotter, J.P. *Organizational Dynamics: Diagnosis and Intervention.* Addison–Wesley Publishing Company, Inc., 1978.

Lawrence, P.R., and J.W. Lorsch. *Organization and Environment: Managing Differentiation and Integration.* Harvard University Press, 1986.

Levinson, H., J. Molinari, and A.G. Spohn. *Organizational Diagnosis.* Harvard University Press, 1972.

Pfeffer, J., and G.R. Salancik. *The External Control of Organizations: A Resource Dependence Perspective.* Harper and Row Publishers, Inc., 1978.

Selznick, P. *Leadership in Administration: A Sociological Interpretation.* Harper and Row Publishers, 1957.

Thompson, J.D. *Organizations in Action: Social Science Bases of Administrative Theory.* McGraw–Hill Book Company, 1967.

The Nature of Management and Challenges of Management

Beckhard, R., and R. Harris, *Organizational Transitions: Managing Complex Change.* Addison–Wesley, 1977.

Beckhard, R., and W. Pritchard, *Changing the Essence: The Art of Creating and Leading Fundamental Change in Organizations.* Jossey–Bass, Inc., 1992.

Chase, G., and E.C. Reveal, *How to Manage in the Public Sector.* Addison–Wesley, 1983.

Covey, S.R. *Principle-Centered Leadership.* Simon and Schuster, 1991.

Hill, L. *Becoming a Manager: How New Managers Master the Challenges of Leadership.* Harvard Business Review Press, 2003.

Hill, L.A., and K. Lineback, *Being the Boss: The 3 Imperatives for Becoming a Great Leader.* Harvard Business Review Press, 2011.

Kotter, J.P. *Power and Influence: Beyond Formal Authority.* The Free Press, 1985.

Mintzberg, H. *Managing.* Berrett–Koehler Publishers, Inc., 2009.

Paton, R. "What makes an effective association: benchmarking business associations for performance" (July 30, 2009) (summary version, unpublished).

Paton, R., and A. Jelking. "No Name Management for the 90's," *Optimum* (Summer 1994), 34–41.

Schein, E.H. *The Corporate Culture Survival Guide.* Jossey-Bass, Inc., 2009.

Stewart, R. *Choices for the Manager: A Guide to Managerial Work and Behaviour.* McGraw–Hill Book Company UK Limited, 1982.

Studies of Managers

Boyatzis, R., and A. McKee. *Resonant Leadership, Renewing Yourself and Connecting with Others through Mindfulness, Hope and Compassion.* Harvard Business School Press, 2005.

Collins, J. *How the Mighty Fall: And Why Some Companies Never Give In.* HarperCollins Publishers Inc., 2009.

Gabarro, J.J. *The Dynamics of Taking Charge.* Harvard Business School Press, 1987.

Kotter, J.P. *The General Managers.* The Free Press, 1982.

Osbaldeston, The Hon. G.F., P.C., O.C. *Keeping Deputy Ministers Accountable.* McGraw–Hill Ryerson Limited, 1989. (Note: Richard Paton was executive director of this study and drafted this report for Osbaldeston.)

Paton, R. "Middle managers: upscale supervisors or emerging executives," *Institute of Public Administration of Canada*, edited by Peter Aucoin, vol. 32, no. 2 (Summer 1989), pp. 244–60.

Paton, R., and A. Goel. "Managing the impossible: How district managers are effective in India," *The International Journal of Public Sector Management*, vol. 6, no. 1 (1993).

Developing Managers, Operating Style of Managers, and Executive Coaching

Argyris, C., and D.A. Schön. *Organizational Learning: A Theory of Action Perspective.* Addison–Wesley Publishing Company, 1978.

Flaherty, J. *Coaching: Evoking Excellence in Others.* Elsevier, 2010.

Kroeger, O., and J.M. Thuesen. *Type Talk: The 16 Personality Types That Determine How We Live, Love, and Work.* Dell Publishing, 1988.

O'Neill, M.B. *Executive Coaching with Backbone and Heart: a Systems Approach to Engaging Leaders with Their Challenges.* Jossey–Bass, 2000.

About the Author

Richard Paton was born and raised in Renfrew and still regards Renfrew fondly as his hometown. He was an avid Junior "A" hockey player in the 1960s, and a competitive golfer at the Renfrew Golf Course and in Ontario.

Since his education and career started in Renfrew, he chose the General Store Publishing House, located in Renfrew, to publish his first book.

Richard has an MA in Canadian Studies from Carleton University and a MPA from Harvard University. He has taught the Politics of Management course part time over the past twenty-five years in the Masters of Public Policy and Administration Program at Carleton University in Ottawa, Ontario.

His management experience involved a variety of senior executive positions in the federal government, including deputy secretary of the Treasury Board Secretariat. He has been president of the Chemistry Industry Association of Ontario for the past seventeen years.

He lives in Ottawa with his wife, Julia, his son, Michael, and his daughter, Jasmine.

TO ORDER MORE COPIES:

GENERAL STORE PUBLISHING HOUSE INC.
499 O'Brien Road, Renfrew, Ontario, Canada K7V 3Z3
Tel 1.800.465.6072 • Fax 1.613.432.3634
www.gsph.com